VALUING YOURSELF AND OTHERS

CAMBRIDGE ADULT EDUCATION
A Division of Simon & Schuster
Upper Saddle River, New Jersey

Executive Editor: Mark Moscowitz
Project Editors: Laura Baselice, Lynn W. Kloss, Robert McIlwaine
Writer: Theresa Flynn-Nason
Production Manager: Penny Gibson
Production Editor: Nicole Cypher
Marketing Manager: Will Jarred
Interior Electronic Design: Mimi Raihl
Illustrator: Allen Davis
Photo Research: Jenifer Hixson
Electronic Page Production: Mimi Raihl
Cover Design: Mimi Raihl

Printed in the United States of America.

1 2 3 4 5 6 7 8 9 10   99 98 97 96 95

ISBN: 0-8359-4670-3

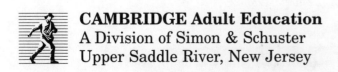
CAMBRIDGE Adult Education
A Division of Simon & Schuster
Upper Saddle River, New Jersey

Contents

Value Yourself

In this unit you will:

- discover the meaning of self-esteem.
- learn to respect yourself.
- build confidence in yourself.

KEY WORDS

self-esteem: your opinion about yourself
self-respect: the value you place on yourself and what you do
self-confidence: a trust in yourself

Meet Ed Santana

Ed Santana is 25 years old. He works at a hardware store. He earns just enough to pay his monthly bills. Sometimes, Ed gets a few hours of overtime. When that happens, he puts a few dollars in the bank.

Ed doesn't drive an expensive car. He doesn't own his own home. He can't go on fancy vacations. A treat for him is a weekend at the beach.

As far as looks go, Ed would be called average. He doesn't have muscles like a sports star. He doesn't have the face of a movie star. He's just a regular guy.

Yet there is something special about Ed. People tend to remember him. He stands out in a group. Other people like to be around him.

Think About It

Think about someone you know who stands out in a group. Check the words below that describe that person.

_____ Friendly   _____ Funny

_____ Kind   _____ Helpful

_____ Good listener   _____ Clever

_____ Interesting   _____ Respects others

_____ Easygoing

What Is Self-Esteem?

What makes Ed Santana special? Ed has high self-esteem. **Self-esteem** is your opinion about yourself. People with high self-esteem like themselves. People with high self-esteem are comfortable with themselves. People with high self-esteem enjoy being who they are.

Ed knows that his life is rather average. He knows that he doesn't have a lot of fancy things. But this doesn't bother Ed. He likes his life. He has a good job. He is healthy. He enjoys being Ed Santana.

Does this mean that Ed thinks that he is better than other people? Absolutely not. High self-esteem does not come from comparing yourself to others. It is not the result of rating yourself against others.

Instead, self-esteem is a personal thing. It is something that comes from deep inside you. It comes from your thoughts and feelings about yourself. It is something that you give yourself.

Think About It

You have just discovered the meaning of self-esteem. Think about the person that you wrote about on the previous page. Do you think that this person has high self-esteem? Explain. (Check your answer on page 118.)

Read each statement. Write T on the answer blank if the statement is true. Write F on the answer blank if the statement is false. (Check your answers on page 118.)

_____1. Self-esteem comes from comparing yourself with others.

_____2. People with high self-esteem like themselves.

_____3. Self-esteem is how you feel about yourself.

_____4. People with high self-esteem think that they are better than others.

_____5. Self-esteem comes from your thoughts and feelings about yourself.

It Wasn't Always That Way

Ed did not always feel good about himself. A few years ago, he felt really lousy about his life. He had just gotten out of high school. He didn't know what to do next. His father was a carpenter. He urged Ed to become a carpenter, too. The money was good. Work was usually available. With his father's contacts, Ed could make a good living.

But there was one problem. Ed wasn't good with his hands. He had trouble putting things together. He had taken shop classes in high school. They had been a nightmare. His projects never turned out right. Ed had struggled to get a passing grade.

Ed didn't want to follow in his father's footsteps. He knew that he wouldn't make a good carpenter. He didn't want to spend his days doing something he didn't enjoy. Yet he let his father talk him into it.

Ed's dad got him a job with his company. Ed tried to go to work with a good outlook. He was always on time. He listened carefully to his boss, Steve. He did whatever he was asked to do. He tried to be a good carpenter, like his dad.

From the first day, Ed had trouble with the job. The simplest task was hard for him. He was always the last one finished. He always needed extra help, and yet he kept making mistakes.

Ed began to hate getting up in the morning. He'd leave the house in a bad mood. He'd stay in a bad mood all day long. He seemed mad all the time. He wasn't fun to be around.

Think About It

What do you think was wrong with Ed?
(Check your answer on page 118.)

Ed's Solution

While shaving one morning, Ed took a good look in the mirror. He didn't like what he saw. The person in the mirror looked angry and unhappy. The person in the mirror was not who Ed wanted to be.

Ed called in sick that day. He went to the park. He lay on a blanket and listened to some music. He thought about his life. He thought about his job. He thought about what his father wanted for him. He thought about what he wanted for himself. Then he went to see his boss, Steve.

Ed gave his notice that day. He told Steve that he just wasn't cut out to be a carpenter. He explained why he had taken the job in the first place. He thanked Steve for helping him.

When Ed was done, Steve smiled. He told Ed he agreed with the decision. It was clear that Ed didn't enjoy the job. It was clear that Ed had struggled with the work. As a matter of fact, Steve thought that he'd have to fire Ed.

Then Steve told Ed about another job. A hardware store from which the company bought materials had an opening. Steve suggested that Ed apply for the job. He'd even write a letter of recommendation for Ed.

When Ed left, he began to whistle. He felt as if a weight had been taken off his shoulders. He felt better than he had in weeks! Now all he had to do was tell his father.

Think About It

Why would Steve offer to write a letter for Ed?
(Check your answer on page 118.)

A New Ed

Although Ed's father was angry for a while, Ed went through with his plans. He got the job at the hardware store. His main duty was waiting on customers. This was something Ed was good at. He always had been a good listener. This skill came in handy in helping the customers. He had seen his dad do all kinds of projects at home. This experience came in handy when a customer needed to know which tools to use. He had always had a good memory. This skill was helpful when he had to find different items in the store.

From the first day, Ed liked his job. He felt good about himself. He felt useful. He felt valuable. Ed's whole outlook changed. He was happier than he had been in a long time.

Think About It

Why was Ed so much happier in his new job?
(Check your answer on page 118.)

The Power of Self-Esteem

Ed Santana's story shows the power of self-esteem. Ed did not like his job as a carpenter. He was not good at the work. He made many mistakes. He felt as if he was letting people down.

All these things affected Ed's self-esteem. He did not feel valuable. He did not like himself. He did not have a good opinion of himself.

Ed realized that he needed to change. The first step was meeting with Steve. The next step was finding a job that he could do well. Finally, he had to face his father. These actions were not easy. They took courage and determination.

Was the effort worth it? Definitely. Today, Ed looks forward to work. He likes who he is. He feels valuable. His self-esteem has increased. He likes being Ed Santana.

What About You?

Think about a time when you let someone talk you into doing something. Now answer these questions about that time.

1. What were you talked into doing?

2. Who talked you into doing it?

3. Why didn't you want to do it?

4. How did you feel when you did it?

5. How did this experience affect your self-esteem?

6. If you had to do it again, would you act differently? Explain.

What Is Self-Respect?

Everyone is good at certain things and not so good at other things. Ed Santana is a good listener. He knows a lot about how to do projects around the house. He has a good memory. All these skills are useful when working in a hardware store. These skills help Ed do his job well.

At work, Ed does things that he is good at. He feels important and useful. He knows that he is needed. In this job, Ed has self-respect.

When you have **self-respect**, you value yourself and what you do. People with self-respect believe that their actions are honorable. They feel as if they make a difference. They are proud of themselves and what they do.

Does self-respect mean thinking that you are good at everything? Absolutely not. Self-respect is knowing that you are good at some things. It also is knowing that you are not so good at other things. Self-respect is accepting your good and bad points. It is believing that you have the right to be happy. It is believing that you have the right to be yourself.

Check What You've Learned _____

Read each statement. Write T on the answer blank if the statement is true. Write F on the answer blank if the statement is false. (Check your answers on page 118.)

_____ 1. People with self-respect know that they are not good at some things.

_____ 2. A person with self-respect does everything well.

_____**3.** People with self-respect believe that they are better than others.

_____**4.** Self-respect means that you honor yourself.

_____**5.** Self-respect is another person's opinion of you.

What's the Connection?

Self-respect is a key to self-esteem. If you have self-respect, you will also have self-esteem. If you think that you are valuable, you will have a good opinion of yourself.

On the other hand, lack of self-respect will cause low self-esteem. If you think that you do nothing right, you will have a low opinion of yourself.

Ed did not respect himself as a carpenter. That job was hard for Ed. He made a lot of mistakes. As a result, he did not feel valuable or important. He did not have self-respect.

Ed's lack of self-respect caused low self-esteem. He did not have a good opinion of himself. He did not like himself.

The job change brought Ed self-respect. He learned that he was very good at certain things. He learned that he could make a difference. He honored himself and his actions. This self-respect caused a rise in his self-esteem. Today, he has a good opinion of himself. He likes being Ed Santana.

Think About It _____

In your own words, describe the connection between self-esteem and self-respect. (Check your answer on page 118.)

What About You?

Remember that time when you let someone talk you into doing something? You wrote about it in Lesson 1. Think about it again. Then answer these questions in the space provided.

1. Did you feel valuable?

2. Were you proud of yourself?

3. What effect did this experience have on your self-respect?

Now think about something you have done that made you feel really good about yourself. Answer these questions about that time.

4. What did you do?

5. What skills did you use?

6. Did you feel proud of yourself? Explain.

7. What effect did this experience have on your self-respect?

What Is Self-Confidence?

You have discovered that self-respect leads to self-esteem. But there is another key to self-esteem. It is self-confidence. **Self-confidence** is trust in yourself. It is feeling sure of yourself. Self-confidence means believing in yourself.

Self-confidence gives you a feeling of control over your life. It gives you the power to make changes. It gives you the strength to live the life you want to live.

Ed Santana showed self-confidence when he left his job as a carpenter. He believed that he would be good in a different job. He trusted himself and his abilities. He decided to take control over his life. He found the power to change.

Does self-confidence mean never making mistakes? No. Everyone makes mistakes. That's part of being a human being. Self-confidence means forgiving yourself when you do make a mistake. Self-confidence means learning from your errors. It means trying again.

If Ed had lacked self-confidence, he might have stayed with a job he hated. Or, he might have quit and never tried another type of work. Then he would have been unhappy with himself. He would have had a poor opinion of himself. His self-respect and self-esteem would have suffered.

Self-Confidence and Self-Esteem

Self-confidence leads to self-esteem. If you trust yourself, you will be able to handle challenges. You will be able to face problems. You will make decisions that you are comfortable with. You will have power over your life. All these things will increase your opinion of yourself. They will raise your self-esteem.

What About You?

Use this activity to check your level of self-confidence. Read each statement. Think about how well the statement describes you. If it describes you very well, circle 5. If it describes you some of the time, circle 3. If it does not describe you, circle 1.

1. I believe in myself.

5	4	3	2	1
Always		Sometimes		Never

2. I know that I am good at certain things.

5	4	3	2	1
Always		Sometimes		Never

3. When I make a mistake, I forgive myself.

5	4	3	2	1
Always		Sometimes		Never

4. I try to learn from my mistakes.

5	4	3	2	1
Always		Sometimes		Never

5. I have some control over my life.

5	4	3	2	1
Always		Sometimes		Never

Now, add up the numbers you circled and check the chart below.

Score	Meaning
20–25	Your self-confidence is great.
10–19	Your self-confidence is average.
5–9	Your self-confidence is low.

What does your score tell you about your self-confidence?

Unit 1 Review

In this unit:

- You learned that self-esteem is your opinion about yourself. Self-esteem is personal. It comes from your thoughts and feelings about yourself.

- You discovered the importance of self-respect. Self-respect is how much you value yourself. If you feel that you are honorable, you will have a good opinion of yourself. You will have high self-esteem.

- You began building your self-confidence. Self-confidence is believing in yourself. It is knowing that you do some things well. Trusting yourself will raise your self-esteem.

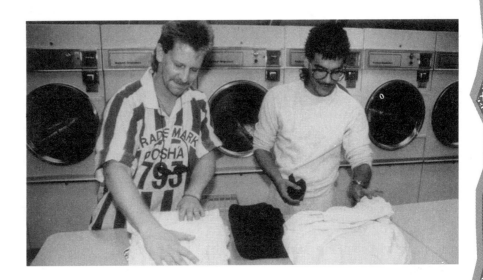

Key Words

Match each word in Column A with the correct meaning in Column B. Write the letter from Column B on the answer blank. (Check your answers on page 118.)

Column A

_____**1.** self-esteem

_____**2.** self-respect

_____**3.** self-confidence

Column B

a. a trust in yourself

b. your opinion about yourself

c. the value you place on yourself and what you do

Key Ideas

Circle the letter of the line that correctly completes each sentence. (Check your answers on page 118.)

1. High self-esteem comes from
   a. comparing yourself to others.
   b. always being better than others.
   c. valuing and trusting yourself.

2. What is a person with high self-esteem like?
   a. self-confident
   b. unfriendly
   c. very smart

3. What is a person with low self-esteem like?
   a. full of self-respect
   b. ready for new challenges
   c. afraid to make changes

4. People who know that they are bad at some things
   a. have low self-esteem.
   b. can still have self-respect.
   c. do not respect others.

5. Self-respect leads to
   a. high self-esteem.
   b. low self-esteem.
   c. selfishness.

6. People with self-confidence
   a. never make mistakes.
   b. feel sure of themselves.
   c. are better than other people.

7. Self-confidence leads to
   a. high self-esteem.
   b. low self-esteem.
   c. selfishness.

What About You?

You have just read about self-esteem. Think about your own self-esteem. Then answer these questions. Write your answers in the space provided.

1. How would you describe your self-esteem? Is it high? Is it low? Is it somewhere in between?

2. What are some things that you could do to increase your self-esteem?

14

The Importance of Self-Esteem

In this unit you will:

- recognize how self-esteem affects your daily life.
- identify examples of high and low self-esteem.
- discover the relationship between attitudes and actions.

KEY WORDS

self-fulfilling prophecy: an action that makes a person's
    predictions come true
attitude: state of mind or feelings
negative: harmful
positive: helpful

Meet Shanelle Clark

Shanelle Clark is 18 years old. She works at The Corner
Coffee Shop. She started working there before she quit high
school. She was hired as a part-time dishwasher. The job
wasn't glamorous. Still, Shanelle was happy for the work. She
needed the money to buy clothes and gifts for her family.

Shanelle worked every weekend. By the time she quit
school in her junior year, Shanelle had been promoted. She
had been made a waitress. Her salary increased.

After a while, Shanelle wondered what she should do. She
could stay at the coffee shop. But she also thought about
going back to school. Some of her friends were even going on
to college. Shanelle had thought about going to college, too.
But she had not even finished high school.

Shanelle's problem was reading. She had trouble
understanding what she read. She'd have to read a page over
and over to get the main idea.

Shanelle was much better at working with numbers than
with words. She'd listen to the teacher explain how to solve a
problem. Then she'd look at the numbers. In no time,
Shanelle would get the answer.

Shanelle always enjoyed her math classes. They made her
feel good about herself. Things were just the opposite in the
other classes. They made her feel dumb. They made her feel
as if something was wrong with her.

Think About It

What class have you taken that made you feel good
about yourself?

The Power of Self-Esteem

Shanelle Clark knew that she was good in math. She thought about finding a job in which she could use this skill. Shanelle's uncle was a bookkeeper. She knew that bookkeepers worked with numbers. She decided to learn more about this job.

One day after work, Shanelle went to see her uncle. He worked for a big company downtown. His office was in a modern skyscraper. Shanelle liked her uncle's office. It looked like a scene from a movie. The expensive furniture and computers were very different from The Corner Coffee Shop.

Shanelle asked her uncle all kinds of questions. She learned what he did at work. She learned what kind of hours he put in. She found out what the salary was. She discovered what he liked about his job. She even found out what he disliked about his job.

Finally, Shanelle asked, "What do I have to do to become a bookkeeper?"

"First you need to finish high school. And a college degree would help," her uncle replied. "You could get a two-year degree at the community college. Then you need some work experience. I think I'd be able to help you out there," said her uncle.

A feeling of gloom came over Shanelle. "Will I take only math classes?" Shanelle asked.

"No," replied her uncle. "You will take a lot of math and accounting classes. But you'll also have to take other courses. You'll probably have to take some English classes."

"Do the other classes involve a lot of reading?" Shanelle asked.

"Definitely," her uncle answered.

Shanelle got up from her chair. She thanked her uncle for his time. She left the office quickly. The closer she got to her home, the worse Shanelle felt.

Think About It

Check the reason Shanelle might have been feeling bad. (Check your answer on page 118.)

_____ She was worried about taking math classes.

_____ She was afraid to take classes that involve a lot of reading.

_____ Her uncle wouldn't help her get a job.

Shanelle's Decision

Shanelle thought about the talk with her uncle. She really wished that she could be a bookkeeper. But she knew it meant reading. It meant struggling to complete assignments. It meant feeling dumb.

Shanelle laughed at herself. How could she even think about going to college? She hadn't even gotten through high school. College was for good students. College was for people who could read easily.

Shanelle decided to stay at The Corner Coffee Shop. Many of her friends went to school, but Shanelle worked 40 hours every week. She kept saving her money. She did her job well. After six months, the shop's owner told Shanelle she was the best waitress she had ever had.

But Shanelle kept thinking about her uncle. She'd picture herself sitting behind his desk. She'd picture herself dressed in a suit rather than a uniform. She'd picture herself doing a job she liked. She'd picture herself being happy.

Think About It

Think about what you learned about self-esteem in Unit 1. Use this knowledge to help Shanelle. Write the answer to each question in the space provided. (Check your answers on page 118.)

1. Does Shanelle have self-respect? Explain.

2. You learned that self-confidence is trust in yourself. Do you think that Shanelle has self-confidence? Explain your answer.

3. You learned that self-esteem is your opinion about yourself. Does Shanelle have high or low self-esteem? Explain your answer.

4. Suppose you were a friend of Shanelle's. What advice would you give her?

The Effect of Self-Esteem

Shanelle's unhappiness is tied into her lack of education and her job. She's working at The Corner Coffee Shop for the wrong reason. She doesn't really like the job. But she feels that it's the best she can get. She wishes that she was working in another kind of job. She wishes that she could use her math skills.

Shanelle doesn't value what she is doing. It doesn't matter that her boss thinks she is doing a great job. Shanelle doesn't think so. Her self-respect is suffering. This is affecting her self-esteem.

In order to change, Shanelle must have confidence in herself. She needs to trust her abilities. But her high school experiences have lessened her confidence. She doesn't believe in herself. This also affects her self-esteem.

Shanelle needs to take charge of her life. She needs to believe in her abilities. She needs to forgive herself for her shortcomings. She needs to make a change.

Think About It

The following paragraphs describe some things that Shanelle can do. Read each one. Decide whether the action would help or hurt Shanelle. Write your reactions in the space provided. Be sure to give the reasons you feel this way. (Check your answers on page 118.)

1. A new bank is opening in town. Three bank teller positions are available. Job requirements include a high school diploma or GED, good math skills, and experience dealing with the public. Shanelle is thinking about applying for a job. Do you think she should?

2. An expensive restaurant is looking for waitresses. The salary is guaranteed to be more than Shanelle makes at The Corner Coffee Shop. Job requirements include past experience waiting tables and a recommendation from a current boss. Do you think that Shanelle should apply for the job?

3. The local library is offering a reading class for adult learners. The class will focus on developing reading comprehension skills. Since the class meets two evenings a week, it will not interfere with Shanelle's work schedule. Do you think that she should sign up for the class?

4. One of the waitresses at The Corner Coffee Shop has a son in second grade. The boy is having a lot of trouble with math. His mother is looking for a tutor who will work with her son for one hour a week. She asked Shanelle whether she'd like to do this tutoring. Do you think that Shanelle should take the job?

5. Which of the actions above would help Shanelle the most? Why?

High and Low Self-Esteem

You make choices every day. Some choices, like what to eat for breakfast, are easy. Some choices, like what you want to do with your life, are more difficult.

Self-esteem affects the choices you make. If you have high self-esteem, you believe in yourself. You have a good opinion of yourself. You know that you are good at certain things. You feel as if you can make a difference.

High self-esteem gives you a sense of power. It makes you feel in charge of your life. You believe that you have a right to a good life. You believe that you have the right to be happy.

Does this mean that nothing bad ever happens to people with high self-esteem? Absolutely not. Nobody's life goes exactly as planned. Things happen that you don't expect to happen. Disappointments may occur.

But high self-esteem helps you get over the disappointments. It helps you make changes when they are needed. High self-esteem helps you learn from your mistakes. It gives you the strength to try again.

Low self-esteem has the opposite effect. If you have low self-esteem, you doubt yourself. You wonder whether you can do anything right. You feel as if the whole world is against you. You feel powerless to make changes.

People with low self-esteem don't want to try new things. They feel that they can't do anything right. They quit before ever trying.

Self-esteem is powerful. It can boost you up, or it can hold you down. It can help you get where you want to go. Or it can set up roadblocks. It has a great impact on your life's choices.

What About You?

What is one of the most difficult choices you have faced? What did you decide to do?

Check What You've Learned

Read each paragraph. Decide whether the person shows high or low self-esteem. Then explain how you reached your decision. (Check your answers on page 118.)

1. Miko's girlfriend broke up with him two months ago. He thinks about her often. He feels that he will never find another girl like her. Miko's friend wants to fix him up with his cousin. The friend says that they have a lot in common. But Miko refuses to meet her. He tells his friend it will be a waste of time. Nobody would want to go out with him.

   High or Low Self-Esteem? _____
   Reasons:

2. Some of the people Oksana works with are joining a bowling league. They ask Oksana whether she'd like to be on their team. Oksana has never bowled before. She doesn't really like sports. But she'd like to get out more. She knows the league will be a way of meeting new people. She tells her coworkers that she is a new bowler. Her friends say that they don't mind. She agrees to join the league.

   High or Low Self-Esteem?_____
   Reasons:

3. Kevin is a gas station attendant. All day long, he pumps gas and checks oil. Kevin would rather work on car engines. He always works on his own car. But the shop where he works doesn't do repair jobs. A local trade school offers a program in automotive repairs. Kevin decides to work part-time and take the course.

High or Low Self-Esteem?_____

Reasons:

4 Paige likes to sing. She has a good voice. In high school, she was a member of the chorus. But high school was a long time ago. She hasn't sung in a group for many years. A friend of Paige's is trying out for a local drama club. The club's next show will be a musical. She wants Paige to audition for a part. Paige refuses. She thinks that she is too old to be in a show. She tells her friend, "They will be looking for younger voices than mine!"

High or Low Self-Esteem?_____
Reasons:

5. Al works in the mail room of a large company. He has been doing the same job for the past five years. A supervisor position has become available. Al's coworkers think that he should apply for the job. But Al is not sure. The new job would mean more money. But it would also mean more responsibility. It would mean being the boss. The job would mean a big change in his life. Al doesn't like change. He decides to stick with his present job. He doesn't apply for the supervisor position.

High or Low Self-Esteem?_____
Reasons:

6. Ahmad likes to build things in his spare time. Ahmad made an unusual mailbox for his parents as an anniversary present. Many neighbors commented on the mailbox. They asked where they could buy one like it. Ahmad thought that he might be able to make some money from his hobby. He made a dozen mailboxes. He rented a table at a local crafts show. Within one hour, Ahmad had sold every mailbox.

High or Low Self-Esteem?_____

Reasons:

Change and Self-Esteem

On the last three pages, you read about how self-esteem affected people's actions. Some of these people did not try new things. They were afraid to fail. They figured that they would be safer if they kept doing what they were used to doing. These people had low self-esteem.

Other people tried new things. They believed in their abilities. They were not afraid to fail. These people had high self-esteem.

Change is a part of life. Through change, you grow. You become the person you want to be. High self-esteem gives you the power to make changes. Low self-esteem makes you fearful of change. Your level of self-esteem can help—or hurt—your personal growth.

25

What About You?

How do you view change? Do you have a fear of failure? Or do you hope for success? This rating scale will help you identify how you see change. Read each statement. Circle the number that describes your feelings most of the time. Be as honest as possible.

1. I like trying new things.

5	4	3	2	1
Always		Sometimes		Never

2. I am successful at the things I do.

5	4	3	2	1
Always		Sometimes		Never

3. I am proud of myself when I try something new.

5	4	3	2	1
Always		Sometimes		Never

4. Trying new things helps me enjoy life.

5	4	3	2	1
Always		Sometimes		Never

5. If I try something different and I fail, I forgive myself.

5	4	3	2	1
Always		Sometimes		Never

6. I think that it is better to have tried something and fail than never to have tried at all.

5	4	3	2	1
Always		Sometimes		Never

Now add up your answers and check your score on the chart below.

Score	Meaning
24–30	You hope for success.
12–23	You hope for success, but you also fear failure.
6–11	You fear failure.

What does your score tell you about your feelings about change? Write your answer in the space below.

Attitudes and Actions

Marie is going to take the test for her driver's permit. She's been getting ready for weeks. She's read the manual. Her friends have asked her practice questions. Marie has worked hard to get ready for the test.

Even so, Marie is a nervous wreck. She's keeps telling herself that she won't pass. She remembers struggling with tests in school. She thinks about every test she ever failed. She tells herself that this test will be like the rest. She's definitely going to fail.

Marie finally arrives at the motor vehicles office and sits down to take the test. Her mind goes blank. She can't remember anything. Marie fails the test just as she had predicted.

Think About It

Check the reason Marie failed the test. (Check your answers on page 119.)

_____ She didn't spend enough time getting ready for it.

_____ Her friends asked her too many questions.

_____ She couldn't remember anything because she was very nervous.

Self-Fulfilling Prophecy

Marie knew the information. But she failed the test anyway. What happened?

Marie's **attitude**, or state of mind, caused her to fail. She went into the motor vehicles office expecting to fail. She was nervous. She was worried. She couldn't think clearly. She couldn't recall what she had learned.

Marie's story is a good example of a self-fulfilling prophecy. With a **self-fulfilling prophecy**, there is a relationship between your attitude and your actions. The term *self-fulfilling prophecy* means that believing something will happen can help make it happen.

Marie went into the motor vehicles office believing that she would fail the test. That attitude affected her behavior. She was so nervous that she couldn't remember anything. She wound up failing. In other words, her attitude made her fear come true. She fulfilled her own prophecy of failing.

Think About It

Think about the idea of the self-fulfilling prophecy as you read this story. Then answer the questions. Write your answers in the space provided. (Check your answers on page 119.)

Mack thinks that he is a bad dancer. At his friend's wedding, the bride asks him to dance. Mack gets nervous. But he feels that it would be rude to refuse the bride. He reluctantly gets up. He can feel everyone watching him. He tries to get the beat. But his feet seem to have a will of their own. Suddenly, Mack trips. He winds up on the floor. "I *knew* this would happen!" Mack thinks.

1. What is Mack's attitude about dancing?

2. How does this attitude affect his behavior?

3. How is this an example of a self-fulfilling prophecy?

Positive Attitudes

In both Marie's and Mack's stories, you saw the power of a **negative**, or harmful, attitude. Both people went into a situation with a negative attitude. Their attitudes affected their behavior. Their actions lived up to their attitudes. They showed a negative self-fulfilling prophecy.

But, what happens when you approach a task with a **positive**, or helpful, attitude? Can a self-fulfilling prophecy be positive?

Meet May Sao

May Sao believes that most people are friendly. She smiles at the people she passes on the street. She always says hello to the people in her neighborhood.

May has a positive attitude. She is friendly to others. Her attitude affects their behavior. They smile back at May. They return her greeting. They are friendly to her.

This is an example of a positive self-fulfilling prophecy. May's positive attitude causes positive actions. Her actions make her attitude come true.

Life Is What You Make It

The self-fulfilling prophecy shows the power of your attitude. Attitude is a personal thing. You determine how you will view yourself and others.

Your attitude affects your relationships with others. A positive attitude will bring positive relationships with others. A negative attitude will bring negative relationships with others. In this way, your attitude gives you some control over your life.

Check What You've Learned _____

Read each statement. Write T on the answer blank if the statement is true. Write F on the answer blank if the statement is false. (Check your answers on page 119.)

_____ **1.** Your attitude and actions are related.

_____ **2.** The self-fulfilling prophecy is always negative.

_____ **3.** A positive attitude helps in dealing with others.

_____ **4.** Your attitude has no effect on your behavior.

_____ **5.** A negative attitude has no effect on your relationship with other people.

Unit 2 Review

In this unit:

- You discovered the power of self-esteem. You saw that self-esteem affects the choices you make. You learned that high self-esteem gives you the power to make good choices. Low self-esteem can make you powerless to make wise choices.

- You explored the effect self-esteem has on your willingness to change. You learned that high self-esteem gives you hope for success. Low self-esteem brings about a fear of failure.

- You compared positive and negative attitudes. You saw that a positive attitude can bring about positive behaviors. A negative attitude can cause negative behaviors. You learned that the idea of the self-fulfilling prophecy describes the relationship between attitudes and actions.

Key Words

Match each word in Column A with the correct meaning in Column B. Write the letter from Column B on the answer blank in Column A. (Check your answers on page 119.)

Column A	Column B
_____ 1. attitude	**a.** an action that makes a person's predictions come true
_____ 2. negative	
_____ 3. positive	**b.** helpful
_____ 4. self-fulfilling prophecy	**c.** state of mind
	d. harmful

Key Ideas

Write your answer to each question in the space provided. (Check your answers on page 119.)

1. How does self-esteem affect the choices you make?

2. What effect does self-esteem have on your willingness to make changes?

3. What is the difference between a hope for success and a fear of failure?

4. What is a self-fulfilling prophecy?

5. How can a positive attitude cause positive behavior?

What About You?

You have just read about attitudes and actions. Think about your own attitude. Then answer these questions. Write your answers in the space provided.

1. Would you describe your attitude as positive or negative? Explain.

2. Does your attitude affect your actions? Does it affect the actions of others? Give examples.

Real World Connection

The Watermelon Jacket _____

The school bus slowly moved down the street. Len, the driver, knew that the roads were very slippery. Last night's snow had put a dangerous white coat on the **pavement**. Len had seen three accidents in the past hour. He was going to make sure that his bus wasn't the fourth.

The bad roads weren't the only thing Len had to watch. His bus was loaded with noisy teens. Most of the kids stayed in their seats. They talked to one another about teachers, parents, TV shows, music—you name it. Some kids even worked on last night's homework.

From his seat, Len had a good view of the bus. He could **glance** in the mirror and see all the way to the back. When he stopped at a red light, Len checked the riders. That was the first time he noticed the new boy.

He sat all alone in a seat made for two. He sat **slumped** down low. His head was pointed downward as if he was looking for something on the floor. Nobody talked to him.

Len would not have noticed the boy if it hadn't been for his jacket. It was the color of a ripe watermelon. It was the brightest jacket on the bus.

It also was probably the oldest. The **material** had worn away in some places, leaving little holes. There were small tears in the arms of the jacket. It was **obvious** that this jacket had been worn by many others. The boy was definitely not its first owner.

Seeing the boy made Len think back to his own days in high school. He knew what it was like to have to wear someone else's old clothes. Len used to get his older brother's things. That brother used to get his clothes from yet another brother. By the time Len wore the clothes, they were already four or five years old. They were always too big. They were always ugly.

Len remembered how he felt in those old clothes. They made him feel ugly. They made him feel **ashamed**. They made him feel **worthless**.

Len looked again at the boy. When he looked at the teen, Len saw himself. He saw an **image** of himself a few years earlier.

Len wanted to talk to the boy. He wanted to tell him about his own life. He wanted to let the boy know that the "jacket does not make the man." But he didn't. When the light turned green, Len stopped thinking about the watermelon jacket. He thought about the snow-covered roads.

Key Words

In the story, eight words are in **bold print**. These words are listed below. Circle the letter of the correct meaning for each word. If you have trouble, go back and read the sentence containing the word. Look for clues in the sentence. Use the clues to figure out the word's meaning. (Check your answers on page 119.)

1. **Pavement** means
   a. an open area.
   b. a paved surface.
   c. a person.
   d. wheels on a bus.

2. **Glance** means
   a. something you drink from.
   b. to talk.
   c. to look.
   d. showing kindness.

3. **Slumped** means
   a. standing tall.
   b. kneeling.
   c. walking.
   d. sliding down.

4. **Material** means
   a. sleeves.
   b. cloth.
   c. shoes.
   d. buttons.

5. **Obvious** means
   a. hidden.
   b. impossible.
   c. clear.
   d. difficult.

6. **Ashamed** means
   a. proud.
   b. shy.
   c. beautiful.
   d. embarrassed.

7. **Worthless** means
   a. important.
   b. of no value.
   c. useful.
   d. honorable.

8. **Image** means
   a. likeness.
   b. make-believe.
   c. teenager.
   d. adult.

Check What You've Learned

Circle the letter of the best answer to each question.
(Check your answers on page 119.)

1. What is Len's job?
   a. Teacher
   b. Policeman
   c. Bus driver
   d. Mechanic

2. Why are the roads dangerous?
   a. They are flooded.
   b. They are covered with snow.
   c. Someone left clothes on them.
   d. They are unpaved.

3. How many accidents did Len see?
   a. None
   b. Two
   c. Three
   d. Four

4. Who was on the bus?
   a. Senior citizens
   b. Young children
   c. Len's family
   d. Teenagers

5. Why did Len look in the mirror?
   a. To check the riders
   b. To comb his hair
   c. To see the car behind the bus
   d. To fix his tie

6. What caused Len to notice the new boy?
   a. He was sitting by himself.
   b. He was wearing a colorful hat.
   c. He was making a lot of noise.
   d. He was wearing a bright jacket.

7. What did Len think of when he saw the boy?
   a. His son
   b. His father

c Himself
d. His sisters

8. How did Len feel when he had to wear used clothes?
   a. Proud
   b. Angry
   c. Ashamed
   d. Happy

9. What did Len want to tell the boy?
   a. "The jacket does not make the man."
   b. "A man has to wear nice clothes."
   c. "You need to make some friends."
   d. "Sit straight in the seat."

10. What did Len do when the light turned green?
   a. He talked to the boy.
   b. He bought a jacket.
   c. He made the boy get off the bus.
   d. He paid attention to the slippery roads.

Think About It

Write the answer to each question in the space provided. (Check your answers on page 119.)

1. Do you think that the boy has low or high self-esteem? Explain why.

2. Len wants to tell the boy that "the jacket does not make the man." What does this mean?

3. If you met the boy, what would you tell him?

Self-Esteem Markers

In this unit you will:

- examine symbols and their meanings.

- explore the relationship between extrinsic (outside) rewards and self-esteem.

- identify the importance of intrinsic (inner) rewards.

KEY WORDS

symbol: an object that stands for something else
extrinsic: something that comes from outside you
intrinsic: something that comes from inside you

Meet the D'Alessios

Vince and Barb D'Alessio have been married for five years. For the past two years, the D'Alessios have been saving for a new car. They finally have enough money for a down payment. Now they must decide what car to buy.

Barb's friend is selling a three-year-old car. The car is in good shape. The price is reasonable. The D'Alessios could pay cash for the car. Barb believes that it is a good car, and she thinks that they should buy it.

Vince doesn't want a used car. He wants a new sports car that costs a lot of money. Even with the deposit, it will take the D'Alessios six years to pay off the car.

Barb thinks that six years is too long to be paying for a car. She doesn't want to spend her life making car payments. She'd rather use the money for other things.

But Vince is firm about wanting a sports car. He goes to the car dealer. He takes a car out for a test drive. Just sitting behind the wheel makes Vince happy. The sports car makes him feel important. The sports car makes Vince feel proud of himself.

Vince goes home and tells Barb about the test drive. He explains how he felt when he drove the expensive car. He tells Barb how much he wants it. What can Barb do? She sees how important the car is to her husband. After a long talk, Barb agrees to buy the car.

Think About It

Do you agree with the D'Alessios' decision to buy the car? Explain why or why not.

37

Symbols and Their Meanings

A car means different things to Vince and Barb. Barb looks at a car as a way of getting places. She wants a car she can depend on. She wants a car she can afford. Owning a fancy car is not important to Barb. She'd rather have an average car and have money for other things.

Vince looks at a car in a different way. A car is more than transportation to Vince. A car is a **symbol**, or an object that stands for something else. To Vince, a sports car is a symbol of power. It is a symbol of wealth. It is a symbol of importance.

When Vince is in the sports car, his feelings change. He feels important. He feels valuable. He feels proud of himself. Vince likes feeling this way. He buys the car (the symbol) for the way it makes him feel.

What About You?

1. How would you feel driving an expensive car? Explain.

2. Listed below are other items that are considered valuable. Circle the items that you would like to own.

house	personal computer
fur coat	expensive watch
in-ground pool	customized van
diamond necklace	designer clothes
leather jacket	big-screen TV
cellular phone	digital stereo system

Look at the items you circled. Choose the one item that you would like to own the most. Then write your answers to these questions in the space provided.

3. Which item did you choose?

4. Why would you like to own this item?

5. How would owning this item make you feel?

6. Do you know someone who owns this item? Who?

7. Look at the other items on the list. What do you think of when you read these words? Are they symbols? In the chart below, list five other items like these. Then describe what each one represents to you.

Item	What It Stands For

You Supply the Meaning

Your life is very different from the lives of people around you. You have different life experiences. These experiences make you see things a certain way. The people around you have other life experiences. They see things a different way. As a result, symbols vary from person to person.

Suppose that you were in a terrible accident while riding in a sports car. Your opinion of sports cars would probably be very different from Vince's. A sports car might be a symbol of danger to you. It could be a symbol of fear or sadness. You probably wouldn't think of it as representing power.

A symbol is a personal thing. You are the one who decides what an item stands for. You are the one who decides whether it is important to you.

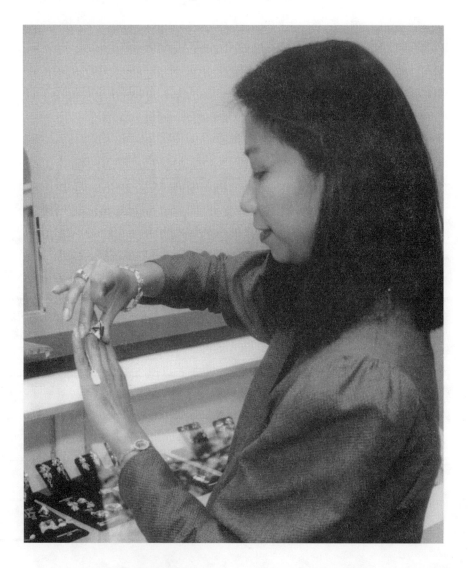

LESSON 8

Extrinsic Rewards and Self-Esteem

Begin here Oct. 25

Vince D'Alessio bought a symbol. He bought the sports car because it stood for something. It made him feel powerful. It made him feel important.

But a car is a thing. It cannot make you feel something. Feelings come from deep inside you. Vince's feelings of importance came from himself, not from the car.

What About You?

Think about a time when you bought a symbol. Then write your answers to the following questions in the space provided.

1. What did you buy?

2. Why did you buy this item?

3. What did it represent to you?

4. How did owning the item make you feel?

5. Did your feelings about the item ever change? Explain.

6. Would you buy the same item again? Why or why not?

It's What Inside That Counts

You have already discovered that self-esteem is your opinion about yourself. People with high self-esteem value themselves. They trust their abilities. They know who they are. They like themselves.

People with high self-esteem do not need fancy things to make them feel good about themselves. Their feelings of self-worth come from inside. They do not need a sports car to feel important. They *know* they are important. They know that their worth as a person has nothing to do with the kind of car they drive.

Vince needed a fancy sports car to feel important. He needed to own a symbol in order to be proud of himself. Vince judged himself by the kind of car he drove.

Think About It

What does Vince's need for a symbol tell you about his self-esteem? (Check your answer on page 119.)

Extrinsic Rewards

Something that comes from the outside is called **extrinsic**. A fancy car is extrinsic. It is something outside of you. The good feelings Vince gets behind the wheel of his car are also extrinsic. They do not come from his opinion of himself. They come from his opinion of a symbol.

Vince needs an extrinsic reward to feel good about himself. This shows that Vince has low self-esteem. He is happy with himself only when he is behind the wheel of his fancy car. There is a problem with this, though. Vince can't stay inside the car all the time. When he is away from his car (the symbol), he will have a low opinion of himself.

Everyone Likes Nice Things

Does wanting to own something special mean that you have low self-esteem? Absolutely not. Everybody likes to own nice things. A fancy car or nice furniture makes life a little more pleasant. Most people work hard to obtain such items. That's normal.

The key is understanding why you want such an item. Do you want the item because it is a good product? Or do you want it because it makes you feel good about yourself? This is the question you need to ask. The answer to this question will then tell you a bit about your own feelings of self-esteem.

Read. Think. Speak.

Check What You've Learned _____

Read about these two people. Use what you know about self-esteem to say whether each person has low or high self-esteem. Then give reasons for your answers. (Check your answers on page 119.)

1. Aimee is saving for a leather jacket. All her friends own one. Whenever she goes out with them, she is embarrassed by her denim coat. She feels that owning a leather jacket will make her more popular.

   Low or High Self-Esteem _____
   Reasons

2. Jeff plays in an adult basketball league. He is the leading scorer on his team. He recently sprained his ankle in a game. Jeff realizes that his old sneakers do not give him enough support. He decides to buy a new pair. The sneakers he wants are the latest rage. What Jeff likes about them is that by pumping them up, he will get extra support.

Low or High Self-Esteem _____
Reasons

Intrinsic Rewards and Self-Esteem

In the last lesson, you read about extrinsic rewards. These are rewards that come from outside you. But not all rewards are extrinsic. Some rewards come from inside you. These rewards are called **intrinsic**.

An intrinsic reward is a personal thing. It is a reward you give yourself. It happens within yourself. Usually, no one else knows about it.

You can think of an intrinsic reward as giving yourself "a pat on the back." You might feel proud that you finished a job. You might feel happy that you helped someone else. You might feel good that you treated someone fairly. Whatever the case, an intrinsic reward is a good feeling that you give to yourself.

Check What You've Learned

Read about each person. Decide whether the reward described is extrinsic or intrinsic. Place a check mark on the blank next to your answer. Then explain your choice in the space below. (Check your answers on page 119.)

1. Tanya works at the post office. She was just named "Employee of the Month."

    _____ Intrinsic reward   _____ Extrinsic reward

2. Inez made a new pair of curtains for her apartment. After hanging the curtains, she stood back and smiled.

    _____ Intrinsic reward   _____ Extrinsic reward

3. Jolette tried out a new recipe. She felt good when it turned out just right.

_____ Intrinsic reward   _____ Extrinsic reward

4. Peter plays on a men's baseball team. He is proud that he drove in the game-winning run.

_____ Intrinsic reward   _____ Extrinsic reward

5. Carlos is pleased that he hasn't had a drink in three weeks.

_____ Intrinsic reward   _____ Extrinsic reward

6. Tyrell is thrilled to learn that he is getting a raise in pay.

_____ Intrinsic reward   _____ Extrinsic reward

Give Yourself a Hand

Do you ever give yourself an intrinsic reward? Maybe you should. Right now, you are reading this book. You are thinking about what you have read. You are completing the activities. You are learning about yourself. You are improving yourself.

Is this easy? No. It takes time. It takes concentration. It takes effort.

When you finish, will you win a big award? Will you get a special prize? No. You are not doing this work in order to receive an extrinsic reward.

You are working through this book for yourself. Your reward is knowing that you took the time to learn some new things. Your reward is pride in yourself. Your reward is feeling good about yourself. Your reward is an intrinsic reward.

Intrinsic rewards raise self-esteem. Intrinsic rewards boost your opinion of yourself. Intrinsic rewards make you happy with yourself.

Only you can give yourself an intrinsic reward. So take a minute now and give yourself a hand.

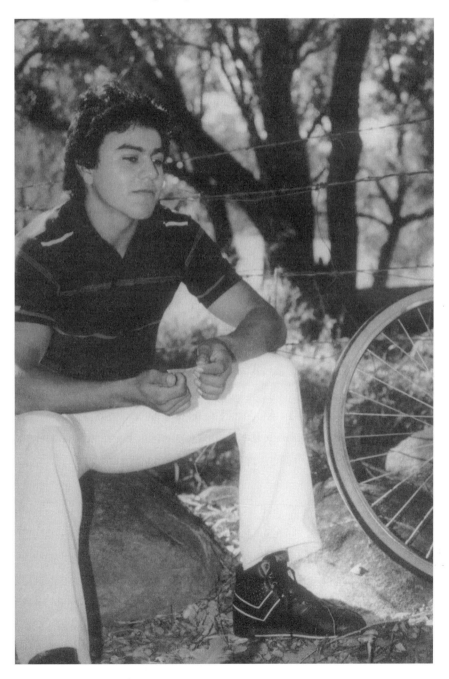

47

Unit 3 Review

In this unit:

- You learned that symbols are things that stand for something. You explored your feelings about different kinds of symbols.

- You discovered the difference between extrinsic and intrinsic rewards.

- You recognized that intrinsic rewards boost self-esteem.

Key Words

Match each word in Column A with the correct meaning in Column B. Write the letter from Column B on the answer blank in Column A. (Check your answers on page 120.)

Column A	Column B
_____ 1. extrinsic	**a.** something that comes from outside you
_____ 2. intrinsic	**b.** an object that stands for something else
_____ 3. symbol	**c.** something that comes from inside you

Key Ideas

Write the answer to each question in the space provided. (Check your answers on page 120.)

1. Give an example of a symbol. What does this symbol stand for?

2. Give an example of an extrinsic reward.

3. Give an example of an intrinsic reward.

4. What effect do intrinsic rewards have on self-esteem?

What About You?

You have just read about rewards and self-esteem. Think about the rewards you have received. Think about how they affected your self-esteem. Then write your answers to the following questions in the space provided.

1. Describe a time when you felt really proud of yourself.

2. What made you feel this way?

3. Did you receive an extrinsic reward or did you give yourself an intrinsic reward?

4. What kind of reward will you receive for completing this book? Explain.

UNIT 4

Raising Self-Esteem

In this unit you will:

- discover the importance of looking at yourself in a realistic way.

- learn how exercise affects self-esteem.

- explore how being positive affects self-esteem.

Key Words

realistic: seeing the truth
message: information passed from one person to another
body language: messages sent by actions of your body

Meet Kayla Longman

Kayla Longman is a single parent. Her days are long and hard. Every morning her alarm rings at 5 A.M. Kayla gets herself ready for work. Then she wakes her baby daughter. She feeds the baby and packs the diaper bag. By 6:30 Kayla and the baby are on their way to the day care center. From there, Kayla rushes to her job in a local factory. She puts in an eight-hour shift.

Kayla's workday doesn't end when her shift is over. She takes the bus back to the day care center and picks up the baby. Once home, Kayla has to take care of dinner, dishes, and bath time. Kayla also tries to spend a little time with her daughter. They look at books together. They watch a TV program together. They play a bit.

When the baby is finally asleep, Kayla has a few minutes to herself. Night after night, she plops down in front of the TV. She doesn't have the energy to do anything else.

One night, Kayla's friend Luisa calls. Luisa tells her that a bunch of their old friends from high school are going out that weekend. They want Kayla to join them. Luisa's sister can watch Kayla's daughter. Kayla tells Luisa she'll think about it. She promises to call Luisa back the next evening.

Kayla thinks about Luisa's invitation. It has been a long time since she has been out with friends. Too long. What could she wear? Kayla had gained weight since the baby was born. None of her nice clothes fit. What could she talk about? All Kayla knows about nowadays are work and babies.

Kayla laughs at herself. She is crazy even to think about going out. She doesn't fit in anymore. She is boring. She is unattractive. She is dull. Who would want to be around someone like that?

51

Kayla calls Luisa back. She tells Luisa that she can't go because she has to stay home with the baby. Then Kayla goes back to her spot in front of the TV. As she looks at the screen, Kayla wishes her life was different. She wishes she was like one of the characters on the screen. Those women are pretty. They are thin. They wear nice things. They are interesting. They are happy. They are all the things Kayla isn't.

Think About It

Go over these + take a poll — see which things are left on list.

Do you get caught up in people you see on T.V.?

Think about the characters you see on the TV. How would you describe them? Put a check mark next to the words that tell something about these characters.
(Check your answers on page 120.)

_____ Thin

_____ Smart

_____ Chubby

_____ Dull

_____ Happy

_____ Perfect

_____ Plain

_____ Funny

_____ Attractive

_____ Kind

_____ Boring

_____ Interesting

_____ Tired

_____ Simple

_____ Full of energy

Be Realistic

Kayla Longman spends most of her free time watching TV. The characters she sees are attractive, thin, and young. They wear nice things. They look glamorous. They seem perfect.

But Kayla forgets that these characters are make-believe. They are not real. That's why they can be perfect.

Real people are not perfect. Real people have both good and bad points. They like some things about themselves. They wish they could change other things.

Kayla should not compare herself to TV characters. It is not realistic. **Realistic** means seeing the truth. Characters on TV are not realistic. When Kayla compares herself to these imaginary beings, she is being unfair to herself. She is being unrealistic.

Concentrate on Your Good Points

Kayla needs to look at herself in a realistic manner. She should concentrate on her good points. She needs to think about the things she does well.

One good thing about Kayla is that she's always on time. She's never been late for work. That takes a lot of effort. It's really hard for Kayla. She has to get the baby ready as well as herself. She also has to bring the baby to the day care center before work.

Kayla works hard at being a good mother. She spends some special time with her daughter each day. Kayla arranges her schedule around the baby. She always puts the baby's needs ahead of her own. When it comes to the baby, Kayla is unselfish.

Kayla's appearance has certain good points. She has always had a great smile. Someone once told Kayla that her smile seemed to light up a room.

Many people compliment Kayla on her hair. It is naturally curly. Other people need to get a perm to have hair like that. Kayla's curls come naturally.

Kayla should think about these good points. It would make her feel better about herself. She would have a higher opinion of herself. Her self-esteem would rise.

Think About It

When you need to think things through, it often helps to make a list. Help Kayla focus on her good points. In the space below, list four things about Kayla that she should be proud of. (Check your answer on page 120.)

What About You?

Think about your good points. What things do you do well? What are you proud of? Read the following list. Put a check mark next to the statements that describe you.

_____ I'm usually on time.

_____ I try to be a good partner.

_____ I try to be a good parent.

_____ I'm dependable.

_____ I listen carefully to others.

_____ I have a good sense of humor.

_____ I have great hair.

_____ I am kind to others.

_____ I have a good memory.

_____ I have a great smile.

_____ I exercise regularly.

_____ I have good posture.

_____ I am easy to get along with.

_____ I'm a hard worker.

Which of your good points are not listed above? Write these good points in the space below.

Improve Yourself

You have helped to name Kayla's good points. But there are some things Kayla would like to change about herself. One of these is her lack of friends. Kayla spends all her free time with the baby. It's been quite a while since she went out with adults. Kayla thinks that people her own age would find her dull. She feels as if she doesn't know how to act with adults anymore.

Luckily, Kayla can change this part of herself. She can join some type of club or group. Her first step is to find out about clubs and groups in her community. Perhaps the day care center has a support group for parents. Maybe a club for single parents is located in her community. The factory where she works might even sponsor activities for employees such as a bowling league or women's sports team.

But Kayla has to take the first step. She needs to look for information about local clubs and groups. She needs to stop *thinking* about changing her life. Instead, Kayla should begin *doing* something to change her life.

Will joining a club make Kayla's life wonderful? No. But it will be a step toward improving herself. It will make Kayla feel as if she has some control over her life. This will make Kayla's opinion of herself grow. Her self-esteem will rise.

Check What You've Learned

Read each statement. If the statement is true, write T on the answer blank. If the statement is false, write F on the answer blank. (Check your answers on page 120.)

_____ 1. Everyone has good and bad points.

_____ 2. People with high self-esteem think that they are perfect.

_____ 3. People with high self-esteem don't try to improve themselves.

_____ 4. Thinking about your good points will raise your opinion of yourself.

_____ 5. Working to improve your bad points will raise your self-esteem.

What About You?

Now it's time to think about yourself. Think about ways in which you might try to improve yourself. Think about why you'd like to make these changes. Then read the following questions and write your answers in the space provided.

1. What is one thing you'd like to change about yourself?

2. Why would you like to make this change?

3. What are two things you could do to improve this part of you?

4. Who could help you make this change?

5. How would making this change affect your self-esteem?

Get Physical

Kayla Longman is unhappy with her weight. She is about 10 pounds heavier than she was before the baby. Many of her favorite clothes no longer fit.

Kayla feels unattractive. This causes her opinion of herself to drop. It gives her feelings of low self-esteem.

Kayla needs to make exercise a daily part of her life. The first thing she needs to do is speak with her doctor. She should make sure that there are no medical reasons to stop her from exercising.

Kayla's next step is to develop an exercise program. She must remember to start off slowly. Too much exercise can hurt rather than help her body.

Kayla must make sure that her program fits in with her busy schedule. She must make sure that the program is something she can do. She must be realistic about how much time she can give to exercise.

Kayla might decide to start walking three times a week. She could take the baby. For the first two weeks, she might walk for 15 minutes. Later she could increase her walk to 30 minutes. Gradually, as she increased the amount of time she walked, she could also quicken her step.

Think About It

The following people decided to start an exercise program. Read what each person did. Decide whether the person started exercising the right way. Write your answers in the space provided. (Check your answers on page 120.)

1. Len's old girlfriend will be in town next week. Len wants to lose some weight before he sees her. He decides to jog 3 miles every day for one week. After his first jog, Len's legs ache. He doesn't know whether he'll be able to stick to his plan.

   Did Len:

	YES	NO
Check with his doctor?		
Start off slowly?		
Make a realistic plan?		

   Did Len begin exercising the right way? What would you tell him to do?

2. Marie just joined a softball team at work. The first game is two weeks away. Marie decides to start getting herself in shape. Every morning before work, she takes a brisk walk. The first day she walked for 20 minutes. She adds 5 minutes to her walk every day.

   Did Marie:

	YES	NO
Check with her doctor?		
Start off slowly?		
Make a realistic plan?		

   Did Marie start exercising the right way? What would you tell her to do?

3. Brian went for a checkup. He discovered that he had gained 10 pounds. Brian asked his doctor about starting an exercise plan. The doctor suggested that Brian take up a sport. Brian used to play basketball in high school. So, he decided to join a men's basketball team. After asking around, Brian learned that there was a neighborhood team. Even though it was midseason, the team had an opening. Brian's first game will be on Saturday. The team will play two games in a local tournament.

Did Brian:

	YES	NO
Check with his doctor?		
Start off slowly?		
Make a realistic plan?		

Did Brian start exercising the right way? What would you tell him to do?

Benefits of Exercise

Daily exercise is good for you. Activities such as walking burn up fat in your body. This can help you lose weight. Daily exercise keeps your body fit. It makes you strong.

Exercise also helps your mind. It is a way to let go of negative or unhealthy feelings. Everybody has occasional feelings of anger or sadness. Keeping these negative feelings locked inside you can be harmful. Exercise is a way of letting go of such feelings. It is a way of working through these feelings.

Regular exercise is also a way of raising your self-esteem. If your body looks good, you will have a good feeling about yourself. If your mind feels good, you will have a good feeling about yourself. A fit mind and fit body will raise your opinion about yourself.

Check What You've Learned

Read each statement. If the statement is true, write T on the answer blank. If the statement is false, write F on the answer blank. (Check your answers on page 120.)

_____ 1. You can never exercise too much.

_____ 2. Exercise adds fat to the body.

_____ 3. You can let go of negative feelings through exercise.

_____ 4. Exercise helps your body and your mind.

_____ 5. Daily exercise can raise your self-esteem.

What About You?

1. Think about how exercise affects you. Circle the words that describe how you feel after exercising. You may circle as many words as you want.

   tired   energetic   calm

   happy   sore   healthy

   proud   weary   alive

   fit   pleased   exhausted

2. Look at the words you circled. Do they show that you feel better or worse after exercising? Write your answer in the space below.

3. Has reading about Kayla changed your feelings about exercise? Explain your answer in the space below.

Be Positive

In Unit 2 you learned that attitude is a state of mind. Your state of mind affects how you feel and look. Your attitude affects your self-esteem.

A positive attitude helps to keep self-esteem high. Some people seem to be born with a positive attitude. They think about their good points. They are proud of what they can do. These feelings build self-esteem.

A negative attitude harms self-esteem. It gives people a low opinion of themselves. Some people always seem to have a negative attitude. They think about their weaknesses. They feel as if they do nothing right.

Luckily, changing your attitude is not that hard. A positive attitude will help you feel better about yourself. It will raise your self-esteem.

Focus on Your Strengths

The first step in developing a positive attitude is to think about your good points. In Lesson 10 you made a list of things you do well. Go back and read this list. Be proud of yourself. Always remember that these strengths make you special.

What About You?

One way to develop a positive attitude is by starting each day with a good thought. This activity will help you start the day off right!

Look again at the list on page 54. Choose three statements from the list. Each statement will be your "Thought for Today." Write one statement in the first box below. Write another statement in the second box. Write another statement in the third box. Then begin each of the next three days by remembering your "Thought for Today."

THOUGHT FOR TODAY

DAY 1

My positive thought for today is that I

THOUGHT FOR TODAY

DAY 2

My positive thought for today is that I

THOUGHT FOR TODAY

DAY 3

My positive thought for today is that I

Messages Without Words

A **message** is information you give to others. There are many different ways to send a message. You can talk to another person. When you speak, you use words to send a message. You can write a letter to someone. When you write, you use words to send a message.

You also send messages without talking or writing. You send messages without words. How? You send messages with your body. This is called **body language**.

You use body language every day. A smile sends a message to those around you. It tells others that you are happy. Without any words, your body language tells others how you feel.

Think About It

Listed below are some kinds of body language. Think about the message sent by each kind of body language. Describe the message sent in the space provided. (Check your answers on page 120.)

1. A frown

2. A wink

3. A thumbs-up sign

4. A thumbs-down sign

5. A shrug

Send a Positive Message

Suppose you are at a meeting. In the middle of the meeting, a stranger walks into the room. The person walks with her head up high. She walks with her shoulders back and her chin up.

What message would you get from her body language? This person feels good about herself. You'd probably get the feeling that she thinks she is special.

Suppose another person comes into the room. This person walks with her shoulders pitched forward. She keeps her head down. Her chin is tucked against her body.

What message would you get from her body language? You'd probably think that this person is unsure of herself. You'd probably get the feeling that she is uncomfortable.

Which of these two people would you want to get to know better? Most people would choose the first woman. Why? Her body language sends a positive message to those around her. Her body language shows that she has a positive attitude. Her body language tells others that she has high self-esteem.

Your body language tells others how you feel about yourself. It shows what kind of attitude you have. It is a sign of your opinion about yourself.

Those around you receive a message from your body language. They react to this message. They treat you accordingly. If the message is positive, people will look upon you favorably. If the message is negative, people will look upon you unfavorably.

You can use body language to raise your self-esteem. Stand tall. Walk in a determined way. Hold your head up high. Smile. Others will get a positive message. They will react in a positive way. You will have good feelings about yourself. Your self-esteem will rise.

Check What You've Learned _____

Read each statement. If the statement is true, write T on the answer blank. If the statement is false, write F on the answer blank. (Check your answers on page 120.)

_____ **1.** Attitudes cannot be changed.

_____ **2.** People with positive attitudes know that they are good at certain things.

_____ **3.** A negative attitude has no effect on self-esteem.

_____ **4.** Beginning each day with a positive thought is one way to raise self-esteem.

_____ **5.** Words are the only way you send a message to those around you.

Unit 4 Review

In this unit:

- You discovered that all people have strengths and weaknesses. There are some things you like about yourself. There are other things you would like to change about yourself. Looking at yourself in a realistic way will help raise your self-esteem.

- You learned that daily exercise helps your body and your mind. Exercise keeps your body healthy and helps you work out unhealthy feelings.

- You realized that a positive attitude helps self-esteem grow. Others learn about your attitude from your body language. If your body language shows a positive attitude, others will treat you favorably. This will cause your self-esteem to rise.

Key Words

Match each word in Column A with the correct meaning in Column B. Write the letter from Column B on the answer blank in Column A. (Check your answers on page 120.)

Column A

_____ **1.** body language

_____ **2.** message

_____ **3.** realistic

Column B

a. information passed from one person to another

b. seeing the truth

c. messages sent by actions of your body

65

Key Ideas

Write the answer to each question in the space provided. (Check your answers on page 120.)

1. Is it realistic to compare yourself to characters in a TV show? Explain.

2. How does thinking about your good points help build self-esteem?

3. Do people with high self-esteem ever think about their weaknesses? Explain.

4. How does exercise help the body?

5. How does exercise help the mind?

6. Suppose your friend wanted to start a daily exercise plan. What would you tell your friend to do?

7. How does a person's attitude affect self-esteem?

8. How can you use your body to send positive messages?

What About You?

What are some things that you intend to do to raise your self-esteem?

Value Others

In this unit you will:

- learn to look for likenesses among people.
- realize that each person is unique and special.
- discover how valuing others can make your life better.

KEY WORDS

unique: unusual; special; rare
traits: characteristics
respect: to honor and be courteous to another
communication: giving and receiving messages

Meet Luz Torres

One hot summer day, Luz took her son to the recreation center. She watched him splash around the kiddy pool. He always loved going to the center. It gave him a chance to see other children from the neighborhood.

Luz also enjoyed the center. It gave her a chance to talk with her neighbors. It gave her a chance to find out what was going on in the neighborhood.

Luz sat next to the pool. She looked around at the other parents. Luz knew almost all of these people. They were her neighbors. They were her friends.

Suddenly, something struck Luz's shoulder. She quickly turned. A plastic ball lay behind her. Luz realized that the ball must have hit her. She looked around for its owner.

A little boy stood a few feet away. From the look on his face, Luz knew the ball was his. She got up and brought it over to him.

Luz handed the ball to the child. He did not say a word. He was terrified. He simply grabbed the toy and ran.

A woman called over to Luz. She said something Luz could not understand. Luz looked at the woman. She did not know her.

Luz watched the stranger moved toward her. Immediately, Luz felt tense. "Who is this person?" she wondered. "And what is she doing here?"

Think About It

Circle the letter of the best answer to the question. (Check your answer on page 120.)

1. Why did Luz get tense when the woman moved toward her?
   a. Luz was angry that she had been hit with the ball.
   b. The woman was a stranger to Luz.
   c. Luz wanted to make a new friend.

Look for Likenesses

The woman introduced herself. Her name was Eva Bunthan. Her son was the boy whose ball had struck Luz Torres. Eva apologized. She asked whether Luz had been hurt.

Luz had some trouble understanding Eva. Her English was not good. She spoke with an accent. Luz had never heard anyone speak that way before.

For a minute, Luz thought about walking away. Eva was different. Eva was a stranger. Why should Luz bother talking to a stranger?

Just then, the ball came flying past Luz again. This time, her son was running after it. Her son and Eva's son were playing catch with it.

Luz decided to talk with Eva. She told Eva that she hadn't been hurt. Then she asked Eva where she lived. Eva explained that she had just moved into the neighborhood. She and her family were renting an apartment in the same building where Luz lived.

For the rest of the afternoon, Luz and Eva talked. They found out that they had a lot in common. Both were 27 years old. Both worked at full-time jobs. Each woman had a son. The boys would be going to the same school.

Before leaving the center, Luz gave Eva her phone number. She told Eva to call her if she needed anything. Eva thanked her. The women made plans to meet at the pool the next weekend.

Luz's son seemed to skip all the way home. Luz asked him why he was so happy. "I had a great day," he said. "I met a new boy and we are friends."

Then he looked seriously at his mother. "Do you like meeting new people, Mama?" he asked.

Luz thought for a moment. "I sure do!" she replied.

One World

The trip to the pool taught Luz something. It showed her how to look at other people. It taught her the importance of seeing how people are alike. She learned not to focus on differences.

Think about what happened when Luz first saw Eva. She saw a stranger. She heard a strange language. She saw someone who was different.

Luz got tense. She didn't want to deal with this new person. She wanted to go back to her neighbors. They were familiar. She was comfortable with them because she knew them. They were like her.

Because of her son, Luz spent some time with Eva. She soon realized that Eva was very much like her. They had a lot in common. In fact, Luz has more in common with Eva than she does with many of her neighbors.

Think About It

(Check your answers on page 121.)

1. Listed below are words that describe Luz and Eva. Think about the story you read about the women. Circle the words that describe both women.

   enjoys swimming   speaks another
                            language

   rents an apartment   has a full-time job

   has one child   has a son

   spends time with her child   likes to exercise

2. Look at the items you circled. Do you think that the women are more alike or different? Write your answer in the space provided.

The Danger of Seeing Differences

If her son hadn't been around, Luz probably would not have gotten to know Eva. She would have seen only their differences. This would have stopped Luz from making a friend.

Seeing differences is like putting a wall around you. It stops you from making new friends. It keeps you away from new experiences. It stops you from growing.

Think About It

Read each story. Think about how the people are alike. Then place check marks in the boxes to show what their likenesses are. (Check your answers on page 121.)

1. Jim is single. He shares an apartment with Bill. Bill is a divorced father with two children. Both men play in a neighborhood basketball league. They enjoy the exercise.

	Jim	Bill	Both
Is unmarried			
Has children			
Enjoys basketball			
Likes to exercise			
Lives in an apartment			

2. Carla and Kiyoko are taking an English class at the local high school. English is a second language for both women. Carla works the night shift in a factory. Kiyoko works the night shift in a diner. Carla is married with two children. Kiyoko is a single parent.

	Carla	Kiyoko	Both
Takes a class			
Speaks English as a second language			
Works the night shift			
Is single			
Is married			
Is a parent			

You're Unique

You've just learned about the importance of seeing likenesses. Does this mean that all people are exactly the same? Absolutely not. Each person is **unique** or special.

Think about all the people that you have seen today. Was anyone exactly like you? No. You are like others in some ways. You are different in other ways. You are unique.

No one else lives a life exactly like yours. No one else has the same experiences as you. No one else sees things exactly the way you do. No one else looks exactly the same as you. No one else *is* you.

What About You?

Think about a close friend of yours. You probably share many likenesses. But you are also two unique people. This activity will show just how special you are.

Compare yourself and your friend in the chart below. The first column lists things that make you different from other people. In the second column, describe yourself. In the third column, describe your friend.

	Me	My Friend
Looks		
Place of birth		
Job		
Hobbies		
Favorite food		
Favorite way to spend an evening		
Dream for the future		

Why Are People Different?

You just named ways that you and your friend are different. But do you know what causes these differences?

Some differences are physical. Your sex, eye color, hair color, and skin color are physical differences. These differences are determined by **traits** or characteristics. You were born with a set of traits. These traits determined these physical differences.

Some differences are caused by things that have happened to you. You are the only person who has lived your life. Your childhood was different from that of others. Your work experiences are different from those of others. The things you do every day are different from what others do.

Some differences are caused by the groups you belong to. Your family is one group. Your friends are another group. Your neighborhood and job are other kinds of groups. Each group has its own way of doing things. Each group affects you.

All these differences combine to make you special. Your differences make you unique. Your differences make you *you*.

What About You?

1. Listed below are different kinds of groups. Circle the groups you belong to.

   Family   Religious group

   Sports team   Group of workers

   Group of friends   PTA

   Neighborhood   Band

   Fan club   A class

   Social club   Volunteer group

2. Which group has caused the most changes in you? Explain.

Check What You've Learned

Read each statement. If the statement is true, write T on the answer blank. If the statement is false, write F on the answer blank. (Check your answers on page 121.)

_____ 1. No two people are exactly alike.

_____ 2. Your traits make you unique.

_____ 3. The groups you belong to have no effect on you.

The Importance of Valuing Others

How many people have you talked to today? Was it more than 10? Was it more than 20? Whatever the number, one thing is sure. None of the people you were around is exactly like another.

You share your world with others. They are all unique. They all have differences. On a bus, at a movie, or even in a store, you are around people who are different.

In order to live your life, you need to be able to get along with others. You need to value others. When you value others, you appreciate them for who they are. You understand that differences exist among people.

Show Respect

One way to value others is by showing respect. To **respect** means to honor and be courteous to another person. There are many ways of showing respect for others.

One way to show respect for others is by treating them fairly. Don't judge a person based upon his or her differences. Make an effort to learn more about the person. It is all right to ask questions in a respectful way. This will help you learn about the other person. It will help you find out how you are similar.

Your actions show respect for others. Do you turn away from people who are different? Do you avoid them? These actions send the message, "I don't want to get to know you." They say, "I don't like you because you're different." They tell others that you don't value them.

What About You?

1. Listed below are different kinds of actions. Circle the words that name what you do when you meet someone who is different.

   Look the other way   Talk to the person

   Stare at the person   Introduce myself

   Avoid the person   Shake the person's hand

   Keep quiet   Smile at the person

2. Look at the words you have circled. Do your actions show respect for the other person?

The Power of Words

Like actions, words send messages. The right words tell others that you respect them. Addressing people by name shows respect. It shows that you honor them.

Calling people "you" sends the opposite message. It tells them that they are unimportant. It says that you are too busy to find out their names. It shows that you don't value them.

Teasing hurts others. Nobody likes to be made fun of. Even good-natured teasing shows a lack of respect.

What About You?

Think about the last time someone made fun of you. Circle the words below that describe how you felt.

Embarrassed   Happy

Scared   Friendly

Angry   Proud

Ashamed   Thrilled

Sad   Humiliated

A Better Life

Valuing others can make your own life better. How? When you show others respect, they will react in a positive way. They will give the respect back to you. You will feel valuable. This will cause your opinion of yourself to rise. Your self-esteem will increase.

Valuing others can also lower the amount of stress in your life. You won't think that different means harmful. You will not think of another person as "bad." You won't have negative feelings. You will be calm, not tense. You will avoid stress.

Valuing others can help in **communication**, or giving and receiving messages. If you respect a person, you will listen carefully to what that person says. You will try to understand how that person feels.

Valuing others can lead to new friendships. It will change the way you look at people who are different. You won't think they are strange. You won't stay away from those people. Instead, you will think each of those people is unique. You will be open to these people. You will learn new things. You even might make new friends.

Think About It

What do you think is the main benefit of valuing others? Explain why this is a benefit.

Check What You've Learned

Read each statement. If the statement is true, write T on the answer blank. If the statement is false, write F on the answer blank. (Check your answers on page 121.)

_____ 1. You should show respect only to people who are like you.

_____ 2. Words can show that you respect a person.

_____ 3. Teasing is one way of valuing others.

_____ 4. Valuing others can help your self-esteem to rise.

_____ 5. Valuing others can lead to new friendships.

Unit 5 Review

In this unit:

- You explored the way people are alike rather than different. You found that looking for differences can be harmful to both you and the other person.

- You realized that you are unique. No one else has the exact same traits that you do.

- You discovered that valuing others can make your life better. Showing respect for others can make your own self-esteem rise. Valuing others helps in communication. It can also lead to new friendships.

Key Words

Match each word in Column A with the correct meaning in Column B. Write the letter from Column B on the answer blank in Column A. (Check your answers on page 121.)

Column A

_____ **1.** communication

_____ **2.** respect

_____ **3.** traits

_____ **4.** unique

Column B

a. to honor and be courteous to another

b. unusual, special, rare

c. giving and receiving messages

d. characteristics

Key Ideas _____

Write your answer to each question in the space provided.
(Check your answers on page 121.)

1. Why should you look for likenesses in people?

2. Explain how you are unique.

3. What causes people to be different?

4. What does it mean to value others?

5. How can you show respect with words?

6. How can you show respect with actions?

7. Can valuing others help your self-esteem? Explain.

8. How does valuing others lower stress?

What About You? _____

Has working through this unit changed the way you
look at people who are different? Explain.

Real World Connection

The Writing Class _____

Angela nervously looked at the map in her hands. She tried to figure out how to get to the Writing Center. But the college had so many buildings. She hadn't **realized** the college was so big. From the highway, it looked as though there were only two or three buildings. Before today, that was the only **contact** Angela had had with the college. It was **simply** a place she passed on her way to work.

But today was different. Angela was going to take a class. Every Saturday for ten weeks, she would be a student again. She had signed up for a writing class. Angela had read about the class in the local newspaper. The college had offered some classes to people in the

community. It didn't cost any money. All you had to do was prove that you lived in the city.

Angela loved to write. She had kept a diary since she was a young girl. She wrote about the people she knew. She wrote about the things that happened to her. Writing made Angela feel good. It helped her think about her feelings. It helped her keep things straight in her mind.

Angela had signed up for the class. That was a few weeks ago. She had looked forward to the first day. Now it was here. But Angela couldn't figure out where to go.

Finally, she asked someone for directions. He pointed to a large building near the highway. Angela hurried toward the Writing Center. She didn't want to be late for her first class.

After a few wrong turns, Angela found the class. She was nervous when she walked into the room. Most of the seats were **occupied**. Luckily, Angela saw an empty desk at the back of the room. Just as she sat down, the teacher entered the room.

Angela looked around the class. A feeling of **dread** came over her. She realized that she was the oldest person in the class. She was even older than the teacher.

Angela felt silly. "What am I doing here?" she thought. "I'm old enough to be that teacher's mother." She wanted to leave. But she was too embarrassed to get up. Everyone would look at her. Everyone would know that she was different.

Suddenly, a thought popped into Angela's mind. She was different. She was unique. She knew things that younger people did not know. She had life **experiences** that the others lacked.

Angela began to think of her difference as something good. She saw herself as **special**. Then, she began to write her first story.

Key Words

In the story, eight words are in bold print. These words are listed below. Circle the letter of the correct meaning for each word. If you have trouble, go back and read the sentence containing the word. Look for clues in the sentence. Use the clues to figure out the word's meaning.
(Check your answers on page 121.)

1. **Realized** means
   a. forgot.
   b. knew.
   c. left.
   d. moved.
2. **Contact** means
   a. connection.
   b. seeing clearly.
   c. avoiding.
   d. meeting.
3. **Simply** means
   a. many.
   b. old.
   c. pretty.
   d. only.
4. **Community** means
   a. books.
   b. neighborhood.
   c. family.
   d. apartment building.

5. **Occupied** means
   a. broken.
   b. empty.
   c. busy.
   d. filled up.
6. **Dread** means
   a. fear.
   b. happiness.
   c. sorrow.
   d. boredom.
7. **Experiences** means
   a. ordinary.
   b. events.
   c. children.
   d. parties.
8. **Special** means
   a. common.
   b. dull.
   c. unusual.
   d. slow.

Check What You've Learned

Circle the letter of the best answer to each question.
(Check your answers on page 121.)

1. Why is Angela at the college?
   a. She is a teacher.
   b. She needs a map.
   c. She is taking a class.
   d. She wants to look around.

2. What day is it?
   a. Monday
   b. Wednesday
   c. Friday
   d. Saturday

3. What did Angela have to do to take the class?
   a. Pay $100
   b. Prove where she lives
   c. Talk to a teacher
   d. Pass a test
4. What had Angela kept since she was a little girl?
   a. A favorite toy
   b. A diary
   c. An old sweater
   d. Her pet dog
5. How did Angela feel when she walked into the classroom?
   a. Sick
   b. Young
   c. Nervous
   d. Smart
6. Where did Angela sit?
   a. In the front row
   b. Behind the teacher
   c. At the back of the room
   d. Near her friend
7. What did Angela discover when the teacher walked into the room?
   a. The teacher was her friend.
   b. She knew the teacher from high school.
   c. The teacher was older than Angela.
   d. The teacher was younger than Angela.
8. How did Angela feel when she saw the teacher?
   a. Silly
   b. Happy
   c. Proud
   d. Calm
9. What thought popped into Angela's head?
   a. She was young.
   b. She was smart.
   c. She was a great writer.
   d. She was different.
10. What did Angela decide to do?
    a. Leave the room
    b. Write a story
    c. Take another class
    d. Go home

Think About It

Write the answer to each question in the space provided. (Check your answers on page 121.)

1. Do you think that Angela has low or high self-esteem? Explain.

2. At first, Angela thought being different was bad. Explain why she felt this way.

3. How did Angela's feelings about being different change?

UNIT 6

Building Self-Esteem in Others

In this unit you will:

- learn how to give compliments.
- explore good listening skills.
- discover that you are a role model.

Key Words

compliment: a comment that shows praise or respect
role model: someone others look up to and try to be like

Meet Tara Simmons

Tara Simmons has just moved back home with her parents. For the past two years, she had lived in another city. Tara had shared an apartment with her boyfriend. Things didn't work out. They began to argue and fight. They decided to split up. Tara asked her parents whether she could come back home.

They were happy to have Tara home. Her old room was still the same as the day she had moved out. The apartment was still the same. At first, Tara thought things were going to be just like they had been before she left. But she was very wrong.

After her first week home, Tara realized that her mother had changed. She used to take pride in how she looked. She used to keep the apartment tidy. She used to be full of energy.

Things were different now. Some days, her mother would spend much of her time in bed. Sometimes, she'd stay in her robe all day long. She didn't seem to care about how the apartment looked. She rarely cooked.

Tara soon realized that something was wrong with her mother. It didn't take long to find out that she had a drinking problem. She knew that her mother used to have a drink once in a while. If friends were over, she'd have a drink. She'd have a drink with dinner. Sometimes, she'd have a drink when watching TV.

Things were different now. Tara's mother would have her first drink with lunch. She'd keep drinking most of the day. Then she'd pass out.

One night, Tara sat down with her father. She told him about her mother's problem. Tara's father just shook his head. He knew about the drinking. He had tried to talk to his wife. He had tried to get some help for her.

But Tara's mother had refused. She insisted that she was fine. She told her husband that she could stop any time she wanted.

Think About It

Circle the letter of the answer that best completes the sentence. (Check your answer on page 121.)

When Tara moved back home, she discovered that her

a. parents had changed her room.

b. parents argued every night.

c. mother had a drinking problem.

Unit Six: Building Self-Esteem in Others

Take Responsibility

Tara Simmons's father told her that there was nothing they could do. Her mother had to help herself. She would stop drinking only when she admitted she had a problem. He had decided to ignore the problem. He told Tara that she should do the same.

But Tara couldn't. She was angry with her mother. She was disappointed. She was embarrassed.

Tara tried to talk to her mother. It was no use. They had an argument. Tara's mother told her to mind her own business.

The Problem Gets Worse

After the talk, the problem got worse. So did Tara's feelings. She was always in a bad mood. She was grumpy. Nothing seemed to make her happy.

Tara's father noticed the change. One night, he gave Tara a pamphlet. It was about a group for adults whose parents abuse drugs. The group met every week. Tara's father suggested that she join the group.

Tara knew that she needed some help. She didn't know how to deal with her mother. She decided that her dad was right. She decided to go to a meeting.

The night of the meeting, Tara was nervous. She was scared and embarrassed. Twice, she turned around to go home. But then she thought about how unhappy she was. She didn't want to stay miserable. She wanted to have a better life.

Tara forced herself to walk into the meeting. She sat at the back of the room. She listened to other people talk. They spoke about their lives. They told stories about their parents. They described how they felt.

Suddenly, Tara put her hand in the air. The group leader called on her. Tara told everyone about her mother.

She told them about her drinking problem. She even told them how angry she felt.

Then Tara sat back down. She was trembling. She was amazed at herself. She couldn't believe she had told her story to a room full of strangers.

A woman tapped Tara on the shoulder. "I want to thank you," she said. "What you just said describes my own life. I also have a mother with a drinking problem. You talked about many of the same feelings that I have. Just hearing your story made me feel better."

"Thank you," Tara replied. "You have just made me feel better, too."

Think About It

Circle the letter of the answer that best completes the sentence. (Check your answer on page 121.)

Tara went to the meeting to

a. make new friends.

b. learn how to speak to a group.

c. find out how to deal with her mother's problem.

Take the First Step

Tara should be proud of herself. Going to the meeting was hard. She was uncomfortable. She was embarrassed. She really didn't want to be there.

But she did go. Why? Tara took a good look at her life. She saw that her mother's problem was affecting her. She didn't like how she felt. Tara didn't want to be angry all the time. She wanted a better life. She wanted to change. But she needed help in making the change.

Tara took responsibility for her feelings. She admitted to herself how she felt. She recognized the cause of her feelings. She decided to do something about how her mother's drinking was affecting her.

Tara knew that she couldn't make her mother stop drinking. Only her mother could do that. But Tara could change how she'd let the problem affect her. Going to the meeting was the first step in making that change.

Tara's actions show high self-esteem. She knows that she is valuable. She knows the kind of life she wants to live. Tara is willing to make changes to have that life. She is willing to take responsibility for herself.

Give Compliments

Taking responsibility for your feelings raises your self-esteem. It can also help build self-esteem in others. How? This happens when you share your feelings with others.

At the meeting, a woman came up to Tara. She said that Tara's words had made her feel good. This woman took responsibility for her feelings. She knew how she felt. She knew why she felt that way. Tara's words made her feel better.

The woman decided to share her feelings with Tara. She complimented Tara. A **compliment** is a comment that shows praise or respect. The woman praised Tara for what she had said to the group. The compliment was honest. It was specific. It was a clear message of what the woman felt.

The compliment helped build Tara's self-esteem. It gave Tara the message "You are special!" It boosted Tara's opinion of herself.

You can help build self-esteem in others by giving compliments. Be sure that your compliments are honest. Be sure that they are specific. Make sure that your words clearly state how you feel about the person. Take responsibility for your feelings—and then share them with others.

Think About It

Read each pair of compliments. Underline the compliment that more clearly shows the speaker's feelings. (Check your answers on page 121.)

1. "You bought a new coat. You look nice in it."

   "I really like your new coat. It shows off the color of your eyes."

2. "Your letter to the mayor was well written. You clearly described the problems at the rec center."

   "I enjoyed reading your letter to the mayor. It was good."

Check What You've Learned

Read each statement. If the statement is true, write T on the answer blank. If the statement is false, write F on the answer blank. (Check your answers on page 121.)

_____ 1. Taking responsibility for your feelings will keep your self-esteem high.

_____ 2. Sharing your feelings with others can help raise their self-esteem.

_____ 3. You should compliment others even if you don't really feel what you say.

Be a Careful Listener

Every day, hundreds of words are spoken to you. You hear the words. But do you *listen* to them?

You might be thinking, "What's the difference between *hearing* and *listening*?" *Hearing* means recognizing sounds. *Listening* means thinking about the sounds. It is a very big difference. It is the difference between talking *at* someone and talking *with* someone.

Listening is an important part of communicating. When you communicate, you use words to send a message to another person. The person hears the words. The person thinks about the words. The person receives your message.

If the person does not listen, he or she does not get the message. Communication stops.

Value Others by Listening

Listening takes time and effort. In order to listen, you have to stop what you are doing. You must concentrate on someone else. You must think about the other person. You must think about the message.

When you listen, you show respect for another person. You show the person that you think he is important. Listening shows that you value the person. This gives the speaker good feelings about him or herself. It helps to boost his or her self-esteem.

Think about a time when you were trying to communicate with another person, but the person was not listening to you. How did you feel? Circle the words below that describe your feelings.

Angry	Proud
Comfortable	Lonely
Sad	Happy
Unworthy	Joyful
Successful	Embarrassed

Let Them Know You Are Listening

There are things you can do to let a speaker know you are listening. First, make eye contact with the speaker. This means looking directly at the person. By looking at the speaker's face, you'll show that you are concentrating on the person.

You can also use body language to show that you are listening. Face the person. Sit up straight or stand tall. This shows that you are paying attention. Nod your head as the person talks. This lets the speaker know that you are thinking about the message.

Words can show the speaker that you are listening. Say things like "Tell me more" or "That's interesting." The words will show support. They will make the speaker feel like you care about her.

What About You?

Think about the last few conversations you've had. Think about your words and your actions. Read each statement below. Circle the number that best describes you during those conversations.

1. I looked at the speaker's face.

5	4	3	2	1
Always		Sometimes		Never

2. I sat up straight or stood tall.

5	4	3	2	1
Always		Sometimes		Never

3. I nodded my head as the person talked.

5	4	3	2	1
Always		Sometimes		Never

4. I used words that showed support for the speaker.

5	4	3	2	1
Always		Sometimes		Never

5. I listened more than I talked.

5	4	3	2	1
Always		Sometimes		Never

Add up the numbers you circled and look at the chart below.

Score	Meaning
20-25	You are a good listener.
11-19	You have some good listening skills.
5-10	You should work on your listening skills.

Respect Others' Opinions

Being a good listener doesn't mean agreeing with everything a speaker says. You can have your own opinion. You can disagree with the speaker.

The key is stating your feelings in a respectful manner. Don't say "You're wrong!" Instead, say "That might be how you feel, but I feel differently." This shows the speaker that you respect his or her opinion, even if you have a different opinion.

Don't make negative remarks. Things like "You're stupid" and "That's the dumbest thing I've ever heard" will stop communication. They will cause bad feelings and lower the self-esteem of the speaker.

Think About It

Read each statement below. If the statement shows respect for the speaker, put a **+** on the line. If the statement is disrespectful, put a **−** on the line. (Check your answers on page 121.)

_____ 1. "I understand how you feel, but I don't agree."

_____ 2. "If you believe that, then you are a real jerk."

_____ 3. "I should have known that you'd be dumb enough to feel that way!"

_____ 4. "You don't have to agree with me. I just feel differently."

_____ 5. "I see why you feel that way. But I still disagree."

Check What You've Learned

Read each statement below. If the statement is true, write T on the answer blank. If the statement is false, write F on the answer blank. (Check your answers on page 121.)

_____ 1. Listening means thinking about what you hear.

_____ 2. A good listener shows respect for others.

_____ 3. Your body language can show a speaker that you are listening.

_____ 4. A good listener always agrees with everything a speaker says.

_____ 5. Listening lowers self-esteem in others.

You're a Role Model

Everybody has role models. A **role model** is someone you look up to. A role model is someone you want to be like. Why? You feel that the person is special. You think that the person has good traits. You think that your life would be better if you were like this person.

Professional sports players are often role models. They are very good at a certain sport. They live a good life. They have nice things. They are famous. Who wouldn't want that kind of life?

What About You?

Think about a famous person who is your role model. Write your answers to the following questions in the space provided.

1. What famous person is your role model?

2. What good traits does this person have?

3. How do you try to be like this person?

Not-So-Famous Role Models

Not all role models are famous. Many are ordinary people. Usually, they don't even know that they are role models. They don't try to be a role model. They just live their lives.

But others notice them. They see their good points. They are impressed. They try to imitate the role model. They try to act like the role model. They try to talk like the role model. They hope to have the same good traits that the role model has.

What About You?

Think of a not-so-famous person who is your role model. Then write your answers to the following questions in the space provided.

1. Who is your role model?

2. What is special about this person?

3. How would being like this person change your life?

You're a Role Model

Did you ever think of yourself as a role model? You are. Other people look up to you. Other people try to imitate you.

If you have children, you are their role model. You are their parent. They look up to you. They try to act like you. They try to be like you.

If you have younger brothers or sisters, you are their role model. They think of you as being older and wiser. They look up to you.

You might be a role model to someone at work—someone who is new on the job or younger than you. You have worked on the job longer than this person has. You are experienced. You have proven yourself.

You might be a role model to someone in your neighborhood. Perhaps the person sees how you live your life. The person thinks that you have good traits. The person tries to be like you.

What About You?

Think about someone who might see you as a role model. Then write your answers to the following questions in the space provided.

1. For whom are you a role model?

2. How does it feel to be a role model? Explain.

3. What good traits do you think the person sees in you?

4. Why would the person want to be like you?

Be a Responsible Role Model

How do you feel now that you know you are a role model? Probably pretty good. It is a compliment to be called a role model. It means that someone sees your good points. It shows that you are respected. It shows that you are valued. It raises your self-esteem.

As a role model, you can help boost the self-esteem of others. How? Act in a way that shows respect for yourself and others. Have a positive attitude. Take responsibility for your feelings. Accept your good and bad traits. Be confident. Believe that you have a right to be yourself.

Others will notice these things. They will try to imitate you. Their self-esteem will grow.

Check What You've Learned

Read each statement. If the statement is true, write T on the answer blank. If the statement is false, write F on the answer blank. (Check your answers on page 121.)

_____ **1.** A role model is someone that others look up to.

_____ **2.** Only famous people are role models.

_____ **3.** Through positive actions, a role model can build self-esteem in others.

Unit 6 Review

In this unit:

- You discovered that compliments can boost the self-esteem of others. A compliment should always be honest. It should clearly describe how the person makes you feel.

- You learned that being a careful listener shows others that you respect them. Eye contact, positive body language, and encouraging words show that you value others.

- You found that you are a role model to others. By acting in a way that shows respect for yourself and others, you can build self-esteem in those around you.

Key Words

Match each word in Column A with the correct meaning in Column B. Write the letter from Column B on the answer blank in Column A. (Check your answers on page 121.)

Column A	Column B
_____ 1. compliment	a. someone others look up to and try to be like
_____ 2. role model	b. a comment that shows praise or respect

Key Ideas

Write the answer to each question in the space provided. (Check your answers on pages 121-122.)

1. How can a compliment boost another person's self-esteem?

2. What is the difference between *hearing* and *listening*?

3. What are three things you can do to show a speaker that you are listening?

4. How does listening affect another's self-esteem?

5. How can a role model boost self-esteem in others?

What About You?

Write the answer to each question in the space provided.

1. What do you think is the most important thing you learned in this unit? Explain.

2. What are some things you intend to do to raise the self-esteem of the people you know?

UNIT 7

Put it Into Practice

In this unit you will:

- review the key ideas of this book.
- practice skills that help raise self-esteem.
- show that you know how to value yourself and others.

Be Proud of Yourself

You have learned a great deal by working through this book. You learned about self-esteem. You discovered how high self-esteem can make your life better. You explored ways of raising your own self-esteem. You even learned ways of raising the self-esteem of others.

Working through this book has taught you new skills. You can use these skills every day of your life. They will help you deal with your feelings. The skills will also help you deal with others.

In this unit you will practice the skills you have learned. The practice will make your skills stronger. The practice will help you learn to value yourself and others.

Reviewing Unit 1: Value Yourself

In Unit 1 you discovered the meaning of self-esteem. You learned how to respect yourself. You began building confidence in yourself.

Think about these things. Look back at Unit 1. Then work through the following activities. They will strengthen the skills you developed in Unit 1.

Think About It

Answer the following questions in the space provided. (Check your answers on page 122.)

1.   Use your own words to describe self-esteem.

2.   Use your own words to describe self-respect.

Check What You've Learned

Circle the words that describe a person who has self-respect. (Check your answers on page 122.)

Proud of his abilities

Never tries to change

Ashamed of his bad points

Is good at some things

Accepts his bad points

Feels needed

Values himself

Feels worthless

Feels as if he makes
a difference

Thinks he is perfect

Think About It

(Check your answers on page 122.)

1. Think about how self-respect and self-esteem are related. Explain how a lack of self-respect can cause low self-esteem. Write your answer in the space provided.

2. Use your own words to describe self-confidence. Write your answer in the space provided.

Check What You've Learned

1. Circle the words that describe a person who has self-confidence. (Check your answers on page 122.)

Learns from his errors

Feels powerful

Is unsure of herself

Takes control of her life

Makes mistakes

Quits if things get hard

Trusts herself

Lacks good points

Runs away from problems

Handles challenges

Think About It

Think about how self-confidence and self-esteem are related. Explain how a lack of self-confidence can lead to low self-esteem. Write your answer in the space provided. (Check your answers on page 122.)

Check What You've Learned

Read each statement. If the statement describes a way to build your self-confidence, put a **+** on the answer blank. If the statement does *not* describe a way to build your self-confidence, put a **–** on the answer blank.
(Check your answers on page 122.)

_____ 1. Remember that you are good at some things.

_____ 2. Feel guilty that you are not good at everything.

_____ 3. Be embarrassed whenever you make a mistake.

_____ 4. Believe that you have the power to make changes.

_____ 5. If you fail at something, never try to do it again.

_____ 6. Learn from your mistakes.

_____ 7. Know that you have the right to live whatever kind of life you want.

_____ 8. Believe in yourself.

_____ 9. Do only those things you know you are good at.

_____ 10. Be ashamed that you are not perfect.

Reviewing Unit 2: The Importance of Self-Esteem

In Unit 2 you discovered how self-esteem affects your daily life. You saw examples of high and low self-esteem. You learned about the relationship between attitudes and actions.

Think about these things. Look back at Unit 2. Then work through the following activities. They will help strengthen the skills you learned in Unit 2.

Check What You've Learned

Read each statement. If the statement is true, write T on the answer blank. If the statement is false, write F on the answer blank. (Check your answers on page 122.)

_____ 1. Self-esteem affects the choices you make.

_____ 2. People with low self-esteem enjoy trying new things.

_____ 3. People with low self-esteem believe in themselves.

_____ 4. High self-esteem gives you a sense of power.

_____ 5. Nothing bad ever happens to people with high self-esteem.

_____ 6. Disappointments happen only to people with low self-esteem.

_____ 7. High self-esteem gives you the strength to try new things.

_____ 8. Low self-esteem can cause you to live a life that you don't like.

Think About It

In Unit 2 you learned that some people have a fear of failure. Other people have hope for success. Use your own words to explain what these terms mean. Write your answers in the space provided.

(Check your answers on page 000.)

1. Fear of failure means

2. Hope for success means

In Unit 2 you compared positive and negative attitudes. Read each statement. If the words show a positive attitude, write P on the answer blank. If the words show a negative attitude, write N on the answer blank. (Check your answers on page 122.)

_____ 1. "I'm going to ask her to go out with me. The worse thing that can happen is she'll say no."

_____ 2. "I don't know why I'm applying for this job. Who would want to hire me?"

_____ 3. "Of course, I didn't win the raffle. I never win anything!"

_____ 4. "I don't know why I keep trying to get ahead. Nothing ever works out right for me."

_____ 5. "With a little work, I know I'll get the job done."

_____ 6. "So I failed the driving test. I'll practice some more and take it again."

_____ 7. "Anything is possible with hard work and determination."

_____ 8. "Who would ever want to go out with me? I'm a mess!"

Reviewing Unit 3: Self-Esteem Markers

In Unit 3 you learned about symbols and their meanings. You explored the relationship between extrinsic rewards and self-esteem. You learned about the importance of intrinsic rewards.

Think about these things. Look back at Unit 3. Then work through the following activities. They will help strengthen the skills you learned in Unit 3.

Check What You've Learned

Read each statement. If the statement is true, write T on the answer blank. If the statement is false, write F on the answer blank. (Check your answers on page 122.)

_____ 1. A symbol is an object that stands for something else.

_____ 2. A symbol has the same meaning for all people.

_____ 3. People with high self-esteem need symbols to feel good about themselves.

Think About It

Read about the following people. Then write your answers to the following questions in the space provided. (Check your answers on page 122.)

Paul wants to buy a car phone. When driving on the highway, Paul sees other drivers talking on their car phones. This impresses Paul. It makes him think that the driver is an important person. Paul wants other people to look at him that way.

1. Why does Paul want a car phone?

2. Do you think that Paul has high or low self-esteem? Explain.

Janeen also wants to buy a car phone. As a salesperson, she drives long distances every day. She's always worried that her car might break down. Janeen thinks that a car phone will keep her safe.

3. Why does Janeen want a car phone?

4. Do you think that Janeen has high or low self-esteem? Explain.

In Unit 3 you compared extrinsic and intrinsic rewards. Use your own words to describe both terms. Write your answers in the space provided.

5. Extrinsic rewards are

6. Intrinsic rewards are

Check What You've Learned _____

Listed below are different kinds of rewards. If the reward is an extrinsic reward, write E on the answer blank. If the reward is an intrinsic reward, write I on the answer blank. (Check your answers on page 122.)

_____ 1. Feeling proud that you finished a job

_____ 2. Being pleased that a meal turned out right

_____ 3. Getting a bonus from your boss

_____ 4. Winning a first-place trophy

_____ 5. Feeling happy that you did a good deed

Reviewing Unit 4: Raising Self-Esteem

In Unit 4 you discovered the importance of looking at yourself in a realistic way. You learned how exercise can affect self-esteem. You found that being positive can build self-esteem.

Think about these things. Look back at Unit 4. Then work through the following activities. They will help strengthen the skills you learned in Unit 4.

Think About It

In your own words, explain what it means to be realistic. (Check your answers on page 122.)

Check What You've Learned

Read about each person. If the person is being realistic, put a **+** on the line. If the person is *not* being realistic, put a **−** on the line. (Check your answers on page 122.)

_____ **1.** Maria wishes that she had expensive clothes like a fashion model.

_____ **2.** Randall thinks that his life would be better if he were as tall as a professional basketball player.

_____ **3.** Kim is dieting to lose 10 pounds.

_____ **4.** Because she wants to be a better dancer, April is taking dance lessons.

_____ **5.** Julio thinks that luck, not hard work, helps a person be successful.

Think About It

In Unit 4 you learned about the benefits of exercise. Read the following questions about exercising. Write your answers in the space provided. (Check your answers on page 122)

1. How does daily exercise help your body?

2. How does daily exercise help your mind?

3. What are three things a person should do when making a daily exercise plan?

4. How does daily exercise help raise a person's self-esteem?

Check What You've Learned

In Unit 4 you learned that you send messages with your body language. Listed below are different kinds of body language. Think about the message sent by each action. If the message is positive, write a **+** on the answer blank. If the message is negative, write a **–** on the answer blank. (Check your answers on page 122.)

_____ **1.** Walking with your head down

_____ **2.** Sitting slumped over in a chair

_____ **3.** Walking with your chin up

_____ **4.** Holding your head up high

_____ **5.** Walking with your shoulders pitched forward

Think About It

Write the answer to each question in the space provided. (Check your answers on page 122.)

1. How is body language a sign of your attitude?

2. How does positive body language help raise self-esteem?

Reviewing Unit 5: Value Others

In Unit 5 you learned to look for likenesses among people. You also realized that every person is unique and special. You discovered that valuing others can make your life better.

Think about these things. Look back at Unit 5. Then work through the following activities. They will strengthen the skills you learned in Unit 5.

Think About It

In your own words, explain why you should look for likenesses among people. (Check your answer on page 123.)

Check What You've Learned

Read each statement. If it describes a likeness, write L on the answer blank. If it describes a difference, write D on the answer blank. (Check your answers on page 123.)

_____ 1. "Our children go to the same school."

_____ 2. "You live in a nicer part of town than I do."

_____ 3. "I exercise every day, but you don't like working out."

_____ 4. "We both take the subway to work."

_____ 5. "We took a class together."

Think About It

(Check your answers on page 123.)

1. In your own words, explain what *unique* means.

2. How are you unique?

Check What You've Learned

Read each statement. If the statement is true, write T on the line. If the statement is false, write F on the answer blank. (Check your answers on page 123.)

_____ **1.** Every person is born with a set of unique traits.

_____ **2.** Your gender and eye color are determined by your traits.

_____ **3.** Your childhood causes you to be different from others.

_____ **4.** The groups you belong to have no effect on you.

_____ **5.** Your differences make you unique.

Think About It

Write the answer to each question in the space provided. (Check your answers on page 123.)

1. How can valuing others help raise your self-esteem?

2. How can valuing others lower the amount of stress in your life?

3. How can valuing others lead to new friendships?

Check What You've Learned

Read each action. If the action shows respect for others, put a **+** on the answer blank. If the action does *not* show respect for others, put a **–** on the answer blank. (Check your answers on page 123.)

_____ **1.** Being courteous to others

_____ **2.** Judging a person based on your differences

_____ **3.** Ignoring a person

_____ **4.** Calling a person "You!"

_____ **5.** Learning about others

_____ **6.** Teasing others

_____ **7.** Asking a person questions about himself or herself

_____ **8.** Addressing a person by name

Reviewing Unit 6: Building Self-Esteem in Others

In Unit 6 you learned how to give compliments. You practiced good listening skills. You discovered that you are a role model.

Think about these things. Look back at Unit 6. Then work through the following activities. They will strengthen the skills you learned in Unit 6.

Check What You've Learned

Read each statement. If the statement is true, write T on the answer blank. If the statement is false, write F on the answer blank. (Check your answers on page 123.)

_____ **1.** A compliment shows respect for another.

_____ **2.** Compliments keep self-esteem low.

_____ **3.** It doesn't matter if a compliment is honest.

_____ **4.** A compliment sends a positive message to another person.

_____ **5.** A compliment should clearly state your feelings.

Read each pair of statements. Underline the statement that is the better compliment.

6. "Your new hairstyle looks nice."

"That hairstyle really shows off the curl in your hair."

7. "You give so much energy to a job that it is a pleasure to work with you."

"I always like working with you."

Think About It

Use your own words to explain the difference between hearing and listening. (Check your answers on page 123.)

Check What You've Learned

Read each action. If it shows that a person is a good listener, put a **+** on the answer blank. If it does *not* show good listening skills, put a **–** on the answer blank. (Check your answers on page 123.)

_____ 1. Telling the speaker that she is dumb

_____ 2. Telling the speaker you don't agree with her

_____ 3. Walking away from the speaker

_____ 4. Interrupting the speaker

_____ 5. Looking at the speaker's face

_____ 6. Nodding as the speaker talks

_____ 7. Saying "Tell me more" to the speaker

_____ 8. Working on something as the speaker talks

Think About It

Write the answer to each question in the space provided. (Check your answers on page 123.)

1. What is a role model?

2. Is it a compliment to be called a role model? Explain why or why not.

3. How can a role model boost the self-esteem of others?

Key Words

Match each word in Column A with the correct meaning in Column B. Write the letter from Column B on the answer blank in Column A. (Check your answers on page 123.)

Column A

_____ 1. attitude

_____ 2. body language

_____ 3. communication

_____ 4. compliment

_____ 5. extrinsic

_____ 6. intrinsic

_____ 7. message

_____ 8. negative

_____ 9. positive

_____ 10. realistic

_____ 11. respect

_____ 12. role model

Column B

a. unusual; special; rare

b. seeing the truth

c. to honor and be courteous to another

d. the value you place on yourself and what you do

e. someone others look up to and try to be like

f. a trust in yourself

g. messages sent by actions of your body

h. an action that makes a person's predictions come true

j. information passed from one person to another

i. state of mind or feelings

_____ **13.** self-confidence

_____ **14.** self-esteem

_____ **15.** self-fulfilling
prophecy

_____ **16.** self-respect

_____ **17.** symbol

_____ **18.** traits

_____ **19.** unique

k. giving and receiving
messages

l. characteristics

m. an object that stands for
something

n. something that comes
from outside you

o. harmful

p. helpful

q. your opinion about
yourself

r. something that comes from
inside you

s. a comment that shows
praise and respect

Key Ideas _____

(Check your answers on page 123.)

1. What are three traits of a person with high self-
esteem?

2. How does self-respect increase self-esteem?

3. How does a positive attitude increase self-esteem?

4. How do intrinsic rewards help keep self-esteem high?

5. How does positive body language help keep self-esteem high?

6. What are two reasons people are different?

7. How can looking for likenesses in people make your life better?

8. How can valuing others make your life better?

9. How does being a careful listener show that you value others?

10. How can a role model raise the self-esteem of others?

What About You? _____

Has working through this book caused any changes in you? Explain.

attitude: state of mind or feelings, 27

body language: messages sent by the actions of your body, 63

communication: giving and receiving messages, 77

compliment: a comment that shows praise or respect, 89

extrinsic: something that comes from outside you, 42

intrinsic: something that comes from inside you, 45

message: information passed from one person to another, 63

negative: harmful, 28

positive: helpful, 29

realistic: truthful, 53

respect: to honor and be courteous to another, 75

role model: someone others look up to and try to be like, 95

self-confidence: a trust in yourself, 11

self-esteem: your opinion about yourself, 3

self-fulfilling prophecy: an action that makes a person's attitudes come true, 28

self-respect: the value you place on yourself and what you do, 8

symbol: an object that stands for something, 38

traits: characteristics, 73

unique: unusual; special; rare, 72

ANSWER KEY

Unit 1: Value Yourself

Think About It (p. 3)
Answers will vary. It is likely that a person who stands out in a group has high self-esteem.

Check What You've Learned (p. 4)
1. F   **2.** T   **3.** T   **4.** F   **5.** T

Think About It (p. 5)
Answers may include: He doesn't like his job; he has a low opinion of himself; he makes many mistakes.

Think About It (p. 6)
Answers may include: Ed had tried to do a good job; he would be a good worker in another field; he never missed a day of work.

Think About It (p. 6)
Ed liked his job. He felt useful. He felt valuable.

Check What You've Learned (pp. 8–9)
1. T   **2.** F   **3.** F   **4.** T   **5.** F

Think About It (p. 9)
Answers will vary. If you think you are valuable and have self-esteem, you will have a good opinion of yourself and self-respect.

Unit 1 Review

Key Words (p. 13)
1. b   **2.** c   **3.** a

Key Ideas (p. 14)
1. c
2. a
3. c
4. b
5. a
6. b
7. a

Unit 2: The Importance of Self-Esteem

Think About It (p. 18)
She was afraid to take classes that involve a lot of reading.

Think About It (pp. 18–19)
1. Shanelle lacks self-respect. She does not value what she does.
2. Shanelle lacks self-confidence. She wants to learn another job. She's afraid to try for it because of her poor reading skills.
3. Shanelle shows low self-esteem. Her actions show that she has a poor opinion of herself.
4. Answers may include: Encouraging Shanelle to find a new job; helping her work on her reading skills; suggesting that she take a reading class.

Think About It (pp. 20–21)
1. No. Shanelle does not have all the necessary qualifications.
2. No. Even though it would be a change, Shanelle would still be a waitress.
3. Yes. The class will help Shanelle develop her poor reading skills.
4. Yes. As a tutor, Shanelle will use her math skills. Helping someone else will probably give Shanelle a better opinion of herself.
5. Taking the reading class will help Shanelle prepare to return to school.

Check What You've Learned (pp. 23–25)
1. Low self-esteem. Miko has a low opinion of himself. Miko thinks that everyone else has the same low opinion of him.
2. High self-esteem. Oksana is willing to try bowling even though she doesn't really like sports.
3. High self-esteem. Kevin wants to change jobs. He's willing to take a class to get the skills necessary for the job he wants.
4. Low self-esteem. Paige has a low opinion of herself. She thinks that she won't make the drama club because of her age.

5. Low self-esteem. Al is not confident in his ability. He's afraid to make a change.
6. High self-esteem. Ahmad recognizes that he has a special talent. He is willing to take a chance on using this talent to earn some money.

Think About It (p. 27)
She couldn't remember anything because she was very nervous.

Think About It (p. 28)
1. Mack has a negative attitude about dancing.
2. He dances poorly.
3. His actions made his thoughts come true.

Check What You've Learned (p. 29)
1. T   2. F   3. T   4. F   5. F

Unit 2 Review

Key Words (p. 30)
1. c   2. d   3. b   4. a

Key Ideas (p. 31)
1. High self-esteem gives you the power to make good choices. Low self-esteem can make you feel powerless to make wise choices.
2. If you have high self-esteem, you have hope for success. You are willing to make changes.
3. People with a fear of failure assume that they will fail at anything they try. They do not believe in themselves. They have low self-esteem. People with a hope for success believe that they will be successful. They know that they are good at some things. They believe in their abilities. They have high self-esteem.
4. The self-fulfilling prophecy describes a relationship between attitudes and actions. It means that it is possible to act in such a way that your thoughts come true.
5. A positive attitude brings about positive relationships with others. As a result of your attitude, you show positive behaviors. Those around you see these behaviors. They react to you in the same way.

Real World Connection: The Watermelon Jacket

Key Words (p. 34)
1. b   2. c   3. d   4. b   5. c   6. d
7. b   8. a

Check What You've Learned (pp. 34–35)
1. c   2. b   3. c   4. d   5. a   6. d
7. c   8. c   9. a   10. d

Think About It (p. 35)
1. Low self-esteem. The boy is ashamed of the way he looks.
2. Clothes do not tell who you really are.
3. Answers may include: Forget the clothes and try to make some friends.

Unit 3: Self-Esteem Markers

Think About It (p. 42)
Vince's need for a fancy symbol shows that he has low self-esteem.

Check What You've Learned (pp. 43–44)
1. Low. Aimee thinks that a leather jacket will make her more popular.
2. High. Jeff wants expensive sneakers because they will give him more support. He doesn't care that they are the latest rage.

Check What You've Learned (pp. 45–46)
1. Extrinsic; Tanya did not give herself this award.
2. Intrinsic, Inez was proud of her curtains.
3. Intrinsic; Jolette's new recipe showed her skill in cooking
4. Intrinsic; Peter was happy that his work won the game.
5. Intrinsic; Carlos is proud that he was able to resist drinking
6. Extrinsic; Tyrell did not raise his own salary.

Unit 3 Review

Key Words (p. 48)
1. a   **2.** c   **3.** b

Key Ideas (p. 49)
1. Answers will vary but may include: a sports car, expensive jewelry, fancy clothes.
2. Answers will vary but may include: getting a raise, winning a prize, receiving a trophy.
3. Answers will vary but may include: feeling good that you helped someone, taking pride in finishing a job, or knowing that you tried as hard as you could.
4. Intrinsic rewards keep self-esteem high.

Unit 4: Raising Self-Esteem

Think About It (p. 52)
Answers will vary but may include attractive, interesting, happy, and perfect.

Think About It (p. 54)
Kayla should be proud that she's always on time, she's a good mother, she has a great smile and nice hair.

Check What You've Learned (p. 55)
1. T   **2.** F   **3.** F   **4.** T   **5.** T

Think About It (pp. 58–59)
1. No, no, no. Len should check with a doctor, start off gradually, and change to a plan that he will be able to follow.
2. No, yes, yes. Marie created a reasonable plan. She might want to check with her doctor.
3. Yes, no, yes. Brian is trying to do too much too fast.

Check What You've Learned (p. 60)
1. F   **2.** F   **3.** T   **4.** T   **5.** T

Think About It (p. 63)
1. Answers may include: "I'm angry" or "I don't like you."
2. Answers may include: "I like to joke" or "I'm attracted to you."

3. Answers may include: "You're OK" or "Everything's great!"
4. Answers may include: "Something's wrong" or "I don't like it."
5. Answers may include: "I don't know" or "I don't care."

Check What You've Learned (p. 64)
1. F   **2.** T   **3.** F   **4.** T   **5.** F

Unit 4 Review

Key Words (p. 65)
1. c   **2.** a   **3.** b

Key Ideas (p. 66)
1. No. Television characters are make-believe and seem perfect. It is unfair to compare yourself to these made up people. You are a human being with good and bad points.
2. It helps keep a good opinion of yourself. This will raise your self-esteem.
3. Yes. They know that they have both good and bad points. They work to improve their weaknesses.
4. Exercise burns fat from the body. This keeps the body strong and fit.
5. Exercise helps you work out negative feelings.
6. Check with your doctor. Start off slowly. Be realistic.
7. A positive attitude increases self-esteem. A negative attitude lowers self-esteem.
8. Positive body language, like walking with your head up high, tells others that you have a good opinion of yourself. Others receive this message and react in a positive manner.

Unit 5 Value Others

Think About It (p. 68)
1. b

Think About It (p. 70)
1. rents an apartment, has a full-time job, has a son, spends time with her child
2. They are more alike.

Answer Key

Think About It (p. 71)
1. Is unmarried, enjoys basketball, likes to exercise, lives in an apartment
2. Takes a class, speaks English as a second language, works the night shift, is a parent

Check What You've Learned (p. 74)
1. T   2. T   3. F

Check What You've Learned (p. 77)
1. F   2. T   3. F   4. T   5. T

Unit 5 Review

Key Words (p. 78)
1. c   2. a   3. d   4. b

Key Ideas (p. 79)
1. Looking for likenesses can help you make new friends and try new things.
2. Answers will vary.
3. People are different because of inherited traits, their past life experiences, and the groups to which they belong.
4. Valuing others means appreciating people for who they are.
5. Addressing a person by his or her name, using words that show respect, avoiding teasing, show respect.
6. Treating people fairly, speaking to people who are different, asking questions to learn about others, showing others that you are interested in them, show respect.
7. When you show others respect, they will react in a positive way. This will increase your self-esteem.
8. You won't be tense or nervous around people who are different from you.

Real World Connection: The Writing Class

Key Words (p. 82)
1. b   2. a   3. d   4. b   5. d   6. a
7. b   8. c

Check What You've Learned (pp. 82-83)
1. c   2. d   3. b   4. b   5. c   6. c
7. d   8. a   9. d   10. b

Think About It (p. 83)
1. Angela has high self-esteem because she made a change in her life and realized she was unique.
2. Angela felt old and left out.
3. She realized that she had special things to offer.

Unit 6: Building Self-Esteem in Others

Think About It (p. 86)
c

Think About It (p. 88)
c

Think About It (p. 90)
1. "I really like your new coat. It shows off the color of your eyes."
2. "Your letter to the mayor was well written. You clearly described the problems at the rec center."

Check What You've Learned (p. 90)
1. T   2. T   3. F

Think About It (p. 94)
1. +   2. -   3. -   4. +   5. +

Check What You've Learned (p. 94)
1. T   2. T   3. T   4. F   5. F

Check What You've Learned (p. 97)
1. T   2. F   3. T

Unit 6 Review

Key Words (p. 98)
1. b   2. a

Key Ideas (p. 99)
1. A compliment shows praise and respect for another person. It helps to raise the person's opinion of him or herself and his or her self-esteem.
2. *Hearing* means receiving sounds. *Listening* is thinking about what you hear.

3. Any of these things: Make eye contact, stand straight, sit tall, say encouraging words can show a speaker that you are listening.
4. Listening shows that you respect the person and his feelings. This increases the person's self-esteem.
5. Others imitate a role model. If the role model shows respect for others, has a positive attitude, and takes responsibility for his or her actions, others will do the same. Their self-esteem will grow.

Unit 7: Put it Into Practice

Think About It (p. 101)
1. Self-esteem is your opinion of yourself.
2. Self-respect is the value you place on yourself and what you do.

Check What You've Learned (p. 102)
Proud of his abilities, is good at some things, accepts his bad points, feels needed, values himself, feels as if he makes a difference

Think About It (p. 102)
1. If you don't value yourself and what you do, then you won't have a good opinion of yourself. You will have low self-esteem.
2. Self-confidence is a trust in yourself.

Check What You've Learned (p. 102)
Learns from her errors, feels powerful, takes control of her life, makes mistakes, trusts herself, handles challenges

Think About It (p. 103)
If you feel powerless to make changes, you will have a low opinion of yourself. You will have low self-esteem.

Check What You've Learned (p. 103)
1. +   2. -   3. -   4. +   5. -
6. +   7. +   8. +   9. -   10. -

Check What You've Learned (p. 104)
1. T   2. F   3. F   4. T   5. F   6. F
7. T   8. T

Think About It (p. 104)
1. Fear of failure means assuming that you will fail at anything you try.

2. Hope for success means thinking that you can be successful at new things.

Check What You've Learned (p. 105)
1. P   2. N   3. N   4. N   5. P
6. P   7. P   8. N

Check What You've Learned (p. 106)
1. T   2. F   3. F

Think About It (pp. 106–107)
1. Paul wants to impress others.
2. Low self-esteem. Paul needs to own a symbol to feel good about himself.
3. Janeen wants to be safe.
4. High self-esteem. She wants the product because it will make her life better.
5. Extrinsic rewards come from your surroundings.
6. Intrinsic rewards are good feelings that you give yourself.

Check What You've Learned (p. 106)
1. I   2. I   3. E   4. E   5. I

Think About It (p. 108)
To be realistic means to be truthful or to see the truth.

Check What You've Learned (p. 108)
1. -   2. -   3. +   4. +   5. +

Think About It (pp. 108-109)
1. Exercise burns off fat, and keeps the body fit and strong.
2. It works out negative feelings.
3. Check with a doctor, begin slowly, be realistic.
4. Exercise keeps the body and mind healthy. This raises self-esteem.

Check What You've Learned (p. 109)
1. -   2. -   3. +   4. +   5. -

Think About It (p. 109)
1. You send messages to others with your body language. Positive messages show that you have a positive attitude.
2. People receive messages from your body language. If the messages are positive, others react to you in a positive way. This raises your self-esteem.

Think About It (p. 110)

Seeing likeness opens up doors to new friendships and new experiences.

Check What You've Learned (p. 110)

1. L **2.** D **3.** D **4.** L **5.** L

Think About It (p. 110)

1. Special; rare; unusual
2. Answers will vary but should list strong points.

Check What You've Learned (p. 111)

1. T **2.** T **3.** T **4.** F **5.** T

Think About It (p. 111)

1. If you value others, they will value you. This will raise your self-esteem.
2. You will not have negative feelings around people who are different from you. You will not be tense or stressful.
3. You will be open to people who are different from you. This makes new friendships and experiences possible.

Check What You've Learned
(pp. 111–112)

1. + **2.** - **3.** - **4.** - **5.** + **6.** -
7. + **8.** +

Check What You've Learned (pp. 112)

1. T **2.** F **3.** F **4.** T **5.** T

6. "That hairstyle really shows off the curl in your hair."
7. "You give so much energy to a job that it is a pleasure to work with you."

Think About It (p. 112)

Hearing is receiving sounds. Listening is thinking about what you hear.

Check What You've Learned (pp. 112-113)

1. - **2.** + **3.** - **4.** - **5.** + **6.** +
7. + **8.** -

Think About It (p. 113)

1. Someone others look up to and try to be like is a role model.
2. Yes. It means that others see your good points and value you.
3. Others imitate a role model. If the role model shows respect for others, has a positive attitude, and takes responsibility for his actions, others will do likewise. This will boost their self-esteem.

Book Review

Key Words (pp. 114-115)

1. i **2.** g **3.** k **4.** s **5.** n
6. r **7.** j **8.** o **9.** p **10.** b
11. c **12.** e **13.** f **14.** q **15.** h
16. d **17.** m **18.** l **19.** a

Key Ideas (pp. 115-116)

1. Answers may include: has self-respect, has self-confidence, values others.
2. People who value themselves have good self-esteem.
3. Focusing on the good things about yourself increases self-esteem.
4. Intrinsic rewards boost your feelings of worth.
5. Positive body language makes people respond positively to you, increasing self-esteem.
6. Different traits, different experiences.
7. It helps you form new friendships and have new experiences.
8. Valuing others improves your relationships and thus your self-esteem.
9. Being a careful listener makes the other person feel important.
10. A role model can provide something good to imitate.

PHOTO CREDITS